UNIVERSITY OF NORTH CAROLINA AT CHAPEL HILL
DEPARTMENT OF ROMANCE LANGUAGES

NORTH CAROLINA STUDIES
IN THE ROMANCE LANGUAGES AND LITERATURES

Founder: URBAN TIGNER HOLMES

Distributed by:

UNIVERSITY OF NORTH CAROLINA PRESS
CHAPEL HILL
North Carolina 27514
U.S.A.

NORTH CAROLINA STUDIES IN THE
ROMANCE LANGUAGES AND LITERATURES

Number 203

THE EVOLUTION OF THE LATIN
/b/ - /u̯/ MERGER

THE EVOLUTION OF THE LATIN /b/ - /u̯/ MERGER:
A Quantitative and Comparative Analysis of the *B-V* Alternation in Latin Inscriptions

BY

JOSEPH LOUIS BARBARINO

CHAPEL HILL

NORTH CAROLINA STUDIES IN THE ROMANCE
LANGUAGES AND LITERATURES
U.N.C. DEPARTMENT OF ROMANCE LANGUAGES
1978

Library of Congress Cataloging in Publication Data

Barbarino, Joseph Louis.
  The evolution of the Latin /b/-/ṷ/merger.

  (North Carolina studies in the Romance languages and literatures; no. 203)
  Bibliography: p.
  1. Latin language—Phonology. 2. Latin language—Consonants. 3. Inscriptions, Latin.
  I. Title. II. Series.

PA2129.B37   471'.5   78-20445
ISBN 0-8078-9203-3

I. S. B. N. 0-8078-9203-3

DEPÓSITO LEGAL: V. 2.660 - 1978   I. S. B. N. 84-499-2028-0
ARTES GRÁFICAS SOLER, S. A. - JÁVEA, 28 - VALENCIA (8) - 1978

TABLE OF CONTENTS

	Page
ABBREVIATIONS, SYMBOLS, AND TERMINOLOGY	9

PART I: INTRODUCTION

1. Nature and Purpose of this Study ... 11
2. Previous Studies of Inscriptional Material ... 12
3. Primary Sources ... 18
4. Areas ... 20
5. Method of Analysis ... 25
6. The *B* and *V* Spelling in Latin Inscriptions ... 27

PART II: THE *B-V* ALTERNATION IN LATIN INSCRIPTIONS: AREAS

7. Britain ... 30
8. The Balkans ... 39
9. Dalmatia ... 50
10. North Africa ... 59
11. Spain ... 75
12. Gaul ... 90
13. Italy ... 104
14. Rome ... 136

PART III: SUMMARY OF FINDINGS AND CONCLUSIONS ... 150

PART IV: THE EVOLUTION OF THE LATIN /b/ AND /u̯/: OTHER SOURCES ... 159

BIBLIOGRAPHY ... 165

ABBREVIATIONS, SYMBOLS, AND TERMINOLOGY

ABBREVIATIONS AND SYMBOLS USED FOR LINGUISTIC FORMS

CLat.	Classical Latin
Fr.	French
It.	Italian
O.	Old
Prov.	Provençal
Roum.	Roumanian
Sp.	Spanish

Capital letters used for whole words indicate Latin forms: BENE, VIXIT.

Italicizing of whole words indicates medieval and modern written forms, usually Romance: Fr. *mon*, Sp. *beso*.

- / /   enclose phonemic symbols: Lat. BENE /bene/, VIXIT /u̯iksit/.
- [ ]   enclose phonetic symbols: Sp. *vino; el vino* [bino]; [el ƀino].
- >   stands for "became": VILLA > Fr. *ville*, Sp. *villa*.
- <   stands for "developed from": Fr. *ville*, Sp. *villa* < VILLA.
- *   stands for hypothetical form: */b/.
- /i̯/:   non-syllabic /i/, always precedes or follows syllabic vowels: CLat. IUVENIS /iu̯u̯enis/.
- /u̯/:   non-syllabic /u/, always precedes or follows syllabic vowels: CLat. VERBIS /u̯erbis/.
- [ƀ]:   voiced bilabial fricative: Sp. *bebe* [beƀe].
- /v/:   voiced labiodental fricative: It. *viene* /vi̯ene/; Eng. *vine* /vai̯n/.

Abbreviations and Symbols Used for Inscriptional Forms

For the sake of clarity, a distinction is made between the vowel symbol *U* and the labiovelar semiconsonant symbol *V*. The heading *(B) → V* used in the tables means that the expected Classical Latin *B* spelling appears as *V*. (And conversely with the headings *(V) → V* and *(V) → B*.)

The following symbols used in the inscriptional examples call for special comment:

a) Letters enclosed in square brackets [ ] are those supplied by the editor, although known to have formed part of a mutilated inscription.

(b) Letters enclosed in parentheses ( ) have been added by the editor to facilitate comprehension, even though nothing is missing on the original stone.

(c) A word appearing in parentheses immediately following a garbled or misspelled form, e.g., PROBARABIT (= PRAEPARAVIT), has been supplied by us for classification.

Inscriptional forms followed only by a number, e.g., BICTOR (= VICTOR) (*D.* 1406) (from the Diehl collection) or VISQUE (= BISQUE) (*V.* 279) (from the Vives collection) are not dated. Forms followed by the letter N, e.g., NOBEM (= NOVEM) (*D.* 1349N), are listed in one of Diehl's frequent notes. Forms followed by any other letter, e.g., IOB. (= IOVIANUS) (*D.* 1970M), are taken from a series of inscriptions.

Terminology

The terms "Vulgar Latin" or "late Latin" will, for the sake of simplicity, refer to the spoken language of the later empire and the following centuries up to the emergence of the Romance dialects.

The terms "correct spelling" or "expected spelling" will, for the sake of simplicity, be used to indicate adherence to the classical norm.

PART I

INTRODUCTION

1. NATURE AND PURPOSE OF THIS STUDY

It is traditionally believed that Classical Latin had two distinct voiced labial phonemes, the voiced bilabial occlusive /b/,[1] and the voiced labiovelar semiconsonant /u̯/. In standard Latin orthography the symbols used to represent the Classical Latin phonemes /b/ and /u̯/ were B and V respectively:

B /b/		V /u̯/	
E. g. LIBENS	/li-bens/	IUVENIS	/iu-u̯e-nis/
ALBA	/al-ba/	SOLVIT	/sol-u̯it/
VERBIS	/u̯er-bis/	SERVUS	/ser-u̯us/
BENE	/be-ne/	VIXIT	/u̯ik-sit/

---

[1] According to Andre Martinet "Some Problems of Italic Consonantism" *Word*, VI (1950), 26-41, in Classical Latin the letter *B* did not represent an occlusive as is generally assumed. He believes that the *B* represented a bilabial fricative /ƀ/. Martinet believes that there was a general weakening of consonants in archaic Latin, which involved, of course, the old occlusive */b/. This became /ƀ/ in archaic Latin. If we accept this hypothesis, Latin had no occlusive /b/ in Classical times; it was already /ƀ/. R. L. Politzer affirms his belief in Martinet's hypothesis in two studies: "On *b* and *v* in Latin and Romance," *Word*, 8 (1952), 211-215 and "On the Fall of Latin -*b*- in Rumanian and Related Phenomena," *Acta Linguistica*, 7 (1952), 32-39.

The indices of the *Corpus Inscriptionum Latinarum* will show an inconsistency in the use of the letters B and V in interior (intervocalic and postconsonantal) and initial positions for the Latin /b/ and /u̯/ in the Latin inscriptions from the greater Empire:

LIVES	(= LIBENS)	IUBENIS	(= IUVENIS)
ALVA	(= ALBA)	SOLBIT	(= SOLVIT)
VERVIS	(= VERBIS)	SERBUS	(= SERVUS)
VENE	(= BENE)	BIXIT	(= VIXIT)

The purpose of the present study is to establish, on the basis of a quantitative-comparative analysis of orthographic deviations from the expected spelling of the B and V, what inferences can plausibly be drawn concerning the status of the original Latin /b/ and /u̯/ from internal evidence of the Latin inscriptions themselves in their geographical and chronological settings. We will investigate Latin inscriptions found in Roman provinces in Britain, the Balkans, North Africa, Dalmatia, Spain, Gaul, and Italy.

2. PREVIOUS STUDIES OF INSCRIPTIONAL MATERIAL

The usefulness of inscriptions as a tool for studying possible dialectical differences in the Latin of the Empire has been adequately demonstrated by previous studies of inscriptional material.[2] We will focus our attention here only on those works which have had a major impact on the design of the present work.

---

[2] The search for dialectical differences in the Latin of the Empire was initiated by Karl Sittl in his work entitled, *Die lokalen Verschiedenheiten der lateinischen Sprache* (Erlangen: Andreas Deichert, 1882). Most of the important works written in the field of inscriptions have been devoted to specific regions, as exemplified by the works of Jules Pirson, *La Langue des inscriptions latines de la Gaule* (Bruxelles, 1901); Albert J. Carnoy, *Le latin d'Espagne d'après les inscriptions*, 2nd ed. (Louvain: J. B. Istas, 1900); Veikko Väänänen, *Le latin vulgaire des inscriptions pompéiennes*, 2nd ed. (Berlin: Akademie-Verlag, 1959; Petar Skok, *Pojave vulgarno-latinskoga jezika na natpisima rimske provincije Dalmacije* (Zagreb: Hartman, 1915); Nunzio Maccarrone, "Il latino delle iscrizioni di Sicilia," *Studi romanzi*, 7 (1911), 75-116.

Studies by E. Diehl, *De m Finali Epigraphica* (Leipzig: B. G. Teübner, 1899); C. Proskauer, *Das auslautende s auf den lateinischen Inschriften*

A. The main comparative, quantitative analysis of the frequency and nature of deviations from the norms of classical Latin orthography in Latin inscriptions in the search of local variations is Paul A. Gaeng's published Columbia University dissertation entitled *An Inquiry into Local Variations in Vulgar Latin as Reflected in the Vocalism of Christian Inscription*.[3] Gaeng studies deviations from the expected spelling of Latin vowels and diphthongs in the collection of Christian inscriptions of Ernst Diehl entitled *Inscriptiones Latinae Christianae Veteres*.[4] This collection contains inscriptions from all areas of the Empire. For Spain, Gaeng used a volume by José Vives entitled *Inscripciones cristianas de la España Romana y Visigoda* because of its more up-to-date material.[5] Gaeng treats inscriptions from Spain, further subdivided into Baetica, Lusitania, and Tarraconensis; Gaul, comprising Gallia Lugdunensis and Gallia Narbonensis; Italy, divided into Northern, Central, and Southern Italy, and Rome, i.e., those areas of the Western Roman World where Romance speech later developed.

B. S. W. Omeltchenko undertook a similar study of the orthographic deviations from the expected spellings of classical Latin vowels and diphthongs in a collection of pagan and Christian inscriptions from the Empire in his 1971 Columbia University dissertation entitled "A Quantitative and Comparative Study of the Vocalism of the Latin Inscriptions of North Africa, Britain, Dalmatia, and the Balkans,"[6] i.e., those peripheral Romanized

---

(Strassburg: Karl J. Teübner, 1909); O. Prinz, *De O et U Vocalibus inter se Permutatis in Lingua Latina* (Halle: Eduard Klinz, 1932); and E. Cross, *Syncope and Kindred Phenomena in Latin inscriptions* (New York: Institute of French Studies, 1930) are among the few studies of inscriptional material that have been of a comparative nature. But it must be noted that these deal with specific phenomena only.

[3] Paul A. Gaeng, *An Inquiry into Local Variations in Vulgar Latin as Reflected in the Vocalism of Christian Inscriptions* (University of North Carolina Studies in the Romance Languages and Literatures, No. 77. Chapel Hill, North Carolina, University of North Carolina Press, 1968).

[4] Ernst Diehl (de.), *Inscriptiones Latinae Christianae Veteres*, 4 vols. (Berlin: Weiderman, 1925-1931).

[5] José Vives, *Inscripciones cristianas de la España Romana y Visigoda* (Barcelona: J. M. Viader, 1942).

[6] Stephen W. Omeltchenko, *A Quantitative and Comparative Study of the Latin Inscriptions of North Africa, Britain, Dalmatia, and the Balkans* (Chapel Hill, N.C.: University of North Carolina Press, 1975).

areas where Latin did not survive in the form of a Romance language (Britain and North Africa), where it did survive (the Balkans) in the form of a Romance language (Roumanian), and where Latin survived (Dalmatia), but a Romance language (Vegliote) is no longer spoken.

C. Not since a study of the *B-V* confusion by J. Parodi [7] has a comparative *étude d'ensemble* of this phenomenon been undertaken on the basis of inscriptions by any Romance scholar. It must be kept in mind, however, that Parodi's study is not based on comparative or quantitative data.

D. The only single work known to the present writer which deals with other important consonantal phenomena, like germination and simplification, the voicing of the intervocalic voiceless stops, palatalization and assibilation, the fall of final consonants, and the phenomenon treated in the present work, on the basis of inscriptions, is an unpublished Ph. D. dissertation written in 1952 by Carl J. Odenkirchen, entitled "The Consonantism of Later Latin Inscriptions: A Contribution to the 'Vulgar Latin Question.'"[8] It would be well to review some of the important features of this work, especially those involving the nature and purpose of the study and the method used to analyze and interpret the data.

In his forward (p. ii), Odenkirchen sets forth his thesis that "The truly popular speech of the centuries in question presented no significant norms or standards, and that the theory of a significant speech unity in pre-Romance popular usage be unequivocally abandoned, and with it such a term as 'Vulgar Latin.'" He chooses to accept the theory advanced by F. G. Mohl,[9] namely, that dialectical differences in the Romance languages go back to an early stage of Vulgar Latin, and to refute that of the

---

[7] J. Parodi, "Del Passagio di *v*- in *b*- e di certe perturbazioni delle legge fonetiche nel latino volgare," *Romania*, 27 (1898), 177-240.

[8] Carl J. Odenkirchen, "The Consonantism of Later Latin Inscriptions: A Contribution to the 'Vulgar Latin' Question" (unpublished Ph.D. dissertation, Department of Romance Languages and Literatures, The University of North Carolina, 1952).

[9] F. G. Mohl, *Introduction à la chronologie du latin vulgaire* (Paris: E. Bouillon, 1899).

INTRODUCTION 15

Franco-American scholar H. F. Muller,[10] who suggested that Vulgar Latin had remained the spoken language of the whole Western Roman Empire until well into the latter part of the eighth century and that at this late period there still existed

> a general unity of speech with a few regional characteristics which do not by any means interfere with the unity of language but are perfectly compatible with it (p. 53).

Whether we choose to accept Muller's theory of a general unity of speech existing in the whole Western Roman Empire until well into the latter part of the eighth century, or to side with Mohl, who advocates an early disruption thereof, an examination of Odenkirchen's work shows that from the point of view of method, he has failed to support the one and to refute the other of these two theories.

Throughout his work, Odenkirchen attempts to present "typical examples of deviations from standard orthography, and then try to determine what phonetic significance the deviations may have" (p. 32), a basic procedure followed in the present work. He wishes his examples to be "representative, not exhaustive; large accumulations of instances ... would serve no useful purpose, and would needlessly increase the length of this study." Forsaking a practical method for a practical consideration, Odenkirchen was apparently unaware that large quantities of data could be efficiently presented in tabular form. We categorically reject, of course, his statement that "Statistical considerations, after all, mean very little. It is obvious that the fact that a certain spelling deviation is found ten times in one region, and fifteen times in those of another, can lead to no valid conclusion..." (p. 33).[11] It

---

[10] H. F. Muller, "A Chronology of Vulgar Latin," *Zeitschrift für romanische Philologie*, Beiheft 78 (Halle: Max Niemeyer, 1929).

[11] Others, in addition to Odenkirchen, have objected to this method. Cf. Frieda N. Politzer and Robert L. Politzer, *Romance Trends in 7th and 8th Century Latin Documents* (University of North Carolina Studies in the Romance Languages and Literatures, No. 21. Chapel Hill, North Carolina: University of North Carolina Press, 1953), p. 35 where these scholars discuss and question the evidence presented by Proskauer and Cross.

has been demonstrated over and over again by Pei,[12] the Politzers,[13] P. Gaeng *(op. cit.)*, S. W. Omeltchenko *(op. cit.)*, and myself that it *is* possible to detect similarities and differences in matters of linguistic development as they may be reflected in the orthography of documentary material (and especially inscriptions), because we believe that these are primarily differences in frequency of occurrence of the same types of phenomena, provided the number of correct occurrences and deviations therefrom are compared in various areas. The failure to show this kind of relationship among the various provinces of the Roman Empire is one of the major criticisms which can be directed against Odenkirchen's work.

He gives us no idea of the size of his corpus, other than to say that he has collected "a very large number of inscriptions" from the entire Roman Empire and has "selected and ordered several thousand of the more pertinent ones" *(ibid.)*.

The possibility of establishing chronological developments on the basis of inscriptions has already been demonstrated by P. Gaeng *(op. cit.)* and S. W. Omeltchenko *(op. cit.)*, and is also made clear from the present work. Odenkirchen makes no attempt to organize his data according to centuries, because, as he says, "by a rough estimate, not more than 10 % of all the inscriptional remains can be assigned a date.... The more informal inscriptions, the crude scratchings or carvings of the nearly illiterate, are usually completely deprived of date, and can often not be placed within a hundred years" (p. 196). Although several scholars have written about matters concerning the dating of inscriptions,[14] a

---

[12] Mario A. Pei, *The Language of the Eighth-Century Texts in Northern France* (New York: Carranza and Co., 1932).

[13] *Romance Trends;* and Robert L. Politzer, *A Study of the Language of the Eighth-Century Lombardic Documents* (New York, 1949).

[14] In Rome and other provinces of the Empire, it was customary to date inscriptions with reference to consuls or emperors in office, or an era of a specific area. See Raymond Bloc, *L'Epigraphie latine* (4th ed.; Paris: Presses Universitaires de France, 1969), pp. 21-32; Emile Hübner (ed.), *Inscriptiones Britanniae Christianae* (Berlin: George Reimer, 1876), p. VIII determines the date of an undated inscription on the basis of its historical content, language, and lettering. He writes: "Tria sunt, unde talis quaestio ordiri potest: res titulis memoratae, sermo eorum, litterarum formae." It is a characteristic feature of Spanish Christian epigraphy to date inscriptions with reference to a specific date. The Spanish

consideration of some figures will easily refute Odenkirchen's generalization. Our figures show that 37.8 % (1,722 dated inscriptions as against 3,015 undated ones) of all inscriptions in our corpus are dated, and that one researcher's generalization can be misleading.

The most serious criticism, which can be directed against Odenkirchen's work, lies in his interpretation of the data. Since the present study is concerned with the Latin intervocalic /b/ - /u̯/ merger, let us re-examine only those sections of his work which treat this phenomenon, since they are representative of his entire approach in many cases. He cites (p. 48) isolated examples of the use of the letter *P* for *B* and interprets these "as a result of a tendency at variance with Romance developments." In another place (pp. 179-180), he cites a number of examples of the use of the letter *F* for an expected *V* spelling, and writes: "These cases of the letter *F* in place of *V*, if they are phonetically reliable, indicate a sound that is at variance with the one that is usually found.... Hence one might take these as examples of a significant variation." Since /b/ did not become /p/, and /u̯/ did not become /f/ in any Romance language, it appears that we are left with an instance where a researcher has confused phonological development with orthographic error.

Odenkirchen's acceptance of Mohl's theory of early dialectalization is a result of his own inclination, and no one would deny him such a persuasion. His attempt, however, to convince us (p. 32) that "Panromanic speech was highly heterogenous" is by no means satisfactory.

E. J. Herman [15] undertook a study of dialectal differences existing in the Latin of the Empire on the basis of inscriptions. Although his analysis is quantitative and comparative, he gives only the total number of deviations from the norms of classical

---

era dates back to the year 38 B. C., so that, for instance, AERA (commonly spelled ERA) DLIIII would mark the year 516 A. D., rather than 554 A. D. Cf. J. Vives, "Características hispanas de las inscripciones visigodas," *Arbor*, 2 (March-April 1944), 186 ff. See also Omeltchenko (pp. 40-44) for a detailed discussion of matters concerning the dating of inscriptions.

[15] J. Herman, "Aspects de la différenciation territoriale du latin sous l'Empire," *Bulletin de la Société de linguistique de Paris*, 60 (1965), 61.

orthography, without any consideration of the frequency of occurrence of correct forms. Herman argues against the use of quantitative data showing the frequency of occurrence of correct forms thus:

> Même si nous mettions en relation le nombre des graphies (= graphie contraire à la norme classique et susceptible de révéler des caractéristiques phonétiques de la langue parlée) avec l'étendue des textes, nous n'obtiendrions rien de linguistiquement valable: la proportion 'graphie fautive/étendue de texte' ne révèle directement que le niveau de la correction orthographique et non pas les caractéristiques de la langue parlée.

It is our belief, however, that important information from the inscriptions can be obtained from a consideration of the frequency of occurrence of correct forms and deviations therefrom. Such is the procedure followed by Gaeng, Omeltchenko, and the present writer.

3. PRIMARY SOURCES

Except for pagan and Christian inscriptions from Britain and pagan inscriptions from the Balkan region, where the paucity of material forced us to turn to other sources for inscriptional matter, Ernst Diehl's collection entitled *Inscriptiones Latinae Christianae Veteres* served as our main source for all inscriptions from other areas. Following is a brief description of the primary sources used in the present quantitative-comparative study of the *B* and *V* in Latin inscriptions from Britain, the Balkans, Dalmatia, North Africa, Spain, Gaul, and Italy:

(1) *The Roman Inscriptions of Britain (Coll.)* by R. G. Collingwood and R. P. Wright served as our source for all of the 486 pagan inscriptions from Britain. This collection is the most up-to-date (the closing date for the inscriptions included December 31, 1954) and comprehensive work ever produced on the Roman inscription of Britain.

(2) For the 77 Christian inscriptions of Britain, we turned to R. A. S. Macalister's *Corpus Inscriptionum Insularum Celti-*

carum (CIIC), published in 1945. Although Emile Hübner's *Inscriptiones Britanniae Christianae*, published in 1876, contains all of the inscriptions (except two) found in the *CIIC*, we have consistently accepted Macalister's reading.[16]

(3) The Latin inscriptions of the *Antike Denkmäler in Bulgarien (Kalinka)* edited by Ernst Kalinka in 1906, were our source for the pagan inscriptions of the Balkans. These inscriptions are from Thracia, Moesia Superior, and Moesia Inferior. Three inscriptions found in this collection are also recorded in Ernst Diehl's corpus of inscriptions (*D.* 434, *D.* 1610, and *D.* 3314).

(4) Ernst Diehl's *(D.) Inscriptiones Latinae Christianae Veteres* was our main source for all of our Christian inscriptions from North Africa (755 inscriptions), Dalmatia (212 inscriptions), Christian Balkan inscriptions (83), and for just two Christian inscriptions from Britain (*D.* 1608), no date, and (*D.* 1820Aa. 685), which are not included in Macalister's volume.

Although the Diehl collection was also our main source for all the Christian inscriptions from Spain (362), Gaul (480), and

---

[16] We accept Macalister's reading over that of Hübner's because of his scholarly and well-documented interpretations and also because the photographs given of each inscriptions are clearer and more revealing than those in Hübner's work, thereby reducing the possibility of misreading. We give here a simple example to show the kind of problem a researcher is confronted with when a certain inscription is recorded in more than one collection and is given variant readings. In Hübner, we have inscription No. 207 recorded as: *loci /sanc/ti Petri apvstoli*. Macalister, on the other hand, gives the following reading for the same inscription (*CIIC*, 519): LOGI T PETRI APVSTOLI. Hübner's reading supposes an *S* to be lost between the *I* (of *loci*) and the *T*, which, according to Macalister (p. 498) is "impossible ... because the stone is here unbroken and shows no trace of writing. It is also quite inadmissible ... to detach the *I* from LOCI turn it into an *S* and read LOC STI (= Sancti)." Macalister *(ibid.)* reads the first word as LOGI, for LOGII, genitive of LOGIUM "dwelling" or "lodging"; and explains the *T* "a sign, a seal, or a mark" with reference to the Vulgate of Ezechiel, ix 4: *signa thau super frontes uirorum gementium:* "mark a *T* on the foreheads of those who lament." The entire inscription may be taken as "The seal of the lodging of Peter the Apostle." See also Omeltchenko's illuminating discussion (pp. 46-47) concerning his acceptance of Macalister's reading of inscription No. 520: *TE DOMINVM · LATINVS ANNORVM XXXV ET FILIA SUA ANNI V IC SINVM FECERVTN* [sic] *NEPVS BARROVADI* over Diehl's reading of the same inscription (*D.* 782): */te/ do/minu/ laudamu. Latinus/ annorum XXXV et filia sua anni V/ .../ iclinum/ fecerunt/ in opus/ Barroua/ di.*

all of Italy (2,183), it had to be supplemented by José Vives' *Inscripciones cristianas de la España Romana y Visigoda*, published in 1942, for Spain, since it includes some 60 inscriptions not found in the Diehl collection.

Diehl's collection consists of three volumes, two of which contain well over 5,000 items from all regions of the Empire where Christian inscriptions were found. The third volume contains extensive indices.

4. AREAS

A detailed description of the inscriptions investigated in the present work, together with some historical data, can be found in P. Gaeng (pp. 28-34) and S.W. Omeltchenko (pp. 51-76). We limit ourselves here to showing the number of inscriptions in each of the areas under investigation, according to centuries. The breakdown of the 4,737 inscriptions used in the present study is as follows:

		PAGAN INSCRIPTIONS		CHRISTIAN INSCRIPTIONS	
Area	Century	No. of Inscr.	Century	No. of Inscr.	
1. Britain	I	17	IV	1	
	II	52	V	12	
	III	88	VI	34	
	IV	23	VII	7	
	n. d.	306	VIII/IX	8	
			n. d.	15	
	Total	486 (37.0 %)*	Total	77 (80.5 %)	
2. Balkans	I	1			
	II	5	IV	5	
	III	13	V	4	
	IV	5	VI	1	
	n. d.	75	n. d.	73	
	Total	99 (24.2 %)	Total	83 (12.0 %)	

---

* The figures in parentheses indicate the percentage of dated inscriptions.

INTRODUCTION

CHRISTIAN INSCRIPTIONS

Area	Century	No. of Inscr.
3. *Dalmatia*	IV	12
	V	24
	VI	9
	n. d.	167
	Total	212 (21.2 %)
4. *No. Africa*	III	7
	IV	54
	V	69
	VI	32
	VII	13
	n. d.	580
	Total	755 (23.2 %)
5. *Spain*		
a) Baetica	IV/VI	54
	VII	36
	n. d.	22
	Total	112 (80.3 %)
b) Lusitania	IV/VI	72
	VII	21
	n. d.	11
	Total	104 (89.4 %)
c) Tarraconensis	IV/VI	68
	VII	46
	n. d.	32
	Total	146 (78.0 %)
6. *Gaul*		
a) Lugdunensis	IV/V	50
	VI/VII	54
	n. d.	110
	Total	214 (31.3 %)
b) Narbonensis	IV/V	23
	VI/VII	61
	n. d.	182
	Total	266 (48.5 %)
7. *Italy*		
a) Northern	IV/V	131
	VI/VII	59
	n. d.	228
	Total	418 (45.4 %)

CHRISTIAN INSCRIPTIONS (Continued)

Area	Century	No. of Inscr.
b) Central	III/IV	55
	V	30
	VI/VII	42
	n. d.	153
	Total	280 (45.3 %)
c) Southern	III/IV	35
	V	41
	VI/VII	79
	n. d.	330
	Total	485 (31.8 %)
8. Rome	III/IV	163
	V	76
	VI/VII	30
	n. d.	731
	Total	1000 (26.9 %)

We are following the formats set down by P. Gaeng and S. W. Omeltchenko concerning the breakdown of inscriptions according to centuries. In his collection of inscriptions Diehl follows the topographical classification of the *Corpus Inscriptionum Latinarum (CIL)*. The volume references for the various areas in the *CIL* are given in parentheses.

A. *Britain (CIL VII)*. Dated pagan inscriptions [17] from this area extend from the first to the fourth centuries although the

---

[17] Because of the paucity of Christian inscriptions in Britain and the Balkans, we were forced to include pagan inscriptions in our study, although they are kept apart from Christian ones, both to increase the size of our corpus from these two areas and to see whether any generalization can be made on the basis of data culled from our investigation of the two kinds of inscriptions. In all other areas only Christian inscriptions are used. According to S. W. Omeltchenko (*op. cit.*, p. 40), "to consider Christian Latin as a special language and the corollary that Christian inscriptions differ unmistakably from pagan inscriptions would be an extremely hazardous assumption." Be that as it may, it would be well to postpone an assumption that the inclusion of pagan inscriptions from these two areas only would, therefore, have no marked effect on our analysis until we have analyzed the data from the two kinds of inscriptions from these areas.

bulk of the material comes from the third century. Dated Christian inscriptions extend from the fourth to the ninth centuries. The bulk of the inscriptions comes from the sixth century. We found one dated Christian inscription from the fourth century. Inscriptions from the fifth, seventh, and eighth/ninth centuries vary in amount from about half a dozen to a dozen.

B. *Balkans (CIL III)*. There are only twenty-four dated pagan inscriptions from the Balkans. These extend from the first to the fourth centuries. Although there is only one dated pagan inscription from the first century, it was decided to keep this as a category in order to parallel the breakdown of pagan inscription from Britain. As can be seen from the tables, dated Christian inscriptions from the fourth, fifth, and sixth centuries are few.

C. *Dalmatia (CIL III)*. The number (45) of dated Christian inscriptions from this region is small. These extend from the fourth to the sixth centuries, and parallel the breakdown of dated Christian inscriptions in the inner Balkans.[18]

D. *Africa (CIL VIII)*. The 175 dated Christian inscriptions from Africa extend from the third to the seventh centuries. The bulk of the material comes from the fourth and fifth centuries.

---

[18] Dalmatia is set off from the rest of the Balkan Peninsula because of its geographical, climatic, and biological characteristics. See Antonio Renato Toniolo's article entitled "Dalmazia," *Enciclopedia Italiana* (Rome: Istituto Giovanni Trecanni, 1931), p. 245.

Historical considerations, which play an important part in historical linguistics generally, seem to have had some importance in shaping the direction of the evolution of Latin in Dalmatia. Concerning this matter, Omeltchenko (p. 70, and note 110) writes: "Most scholars agree that the two historical events that were instrumental in causing the Latin of Dalmatia to develop differently from that of the inland Balkan Peninsula were the Diocletian division towards the end of the third century, whereby the southern part of Dalmatia, with the cities of Lissus, Scodra, and Doclea, was separated from the rest of the province and formed into a new province named Dalmatia Praevalitana, thus included in Illyricum oriental, and the official division in A. D. 395 of the Roman Empire into the eastern and western parts, Dalmatia remaining with Rome and Praevalitana (modern Montenegro and northern Albania) going with Constantinople. Since most of Dalmatia remained under the influence of Rome, it could thus take part in those linguistic evolutions which affected Western Romance, innovations which the Latin of the Eastern Empire did not undergo." In the present study, we will investigate whether the evolution of the Latin /b/ and /u̯/ in Dalmatia differs from that of the inland Balkan Peninsula on the basis of inscriptional material.

E. *Spain (CIL II)*, further subdivided into:

(a) Baetica, (b) Lusitania, and (c) Tarraconensis.

In view of the small number of dated inscriptions in the centuries preceding the sixth in this area, and the small number of specifically dated inscriptions from Tarraconensis, we decided

(1) to treat all dated inscriptions of the fourth, fifth, and sixth centuries as one group and to reserve separate treatment only to inscriptions of the seventh century;
(2) to include in dated material the prose funeral inscriptions found at Tarragona and believed to originate from between the fourth and early sixth centuries.

F. *Gaul*, comprising

(a) Gallia Lugdunensis *(CIL XIII)* and (b) Gallia Narbonensis *(CIL XII)*.

Our inscriptional material from these areas is divided into fourth/fifth and sixth/seventh centuries, although the bulk of dated inscriptions comes from the fifth and sixth centuries. Dated inscriptions from the fourth and seventh centuries are few.

G. *Italy*, divided into

(a) Northern *(CIL V)*, (b) Central *(CIL, XI)*, and
(c) Southern.

This last region includes inscriptions scattered over three volumes of the Corpus *(CIL IX, CIL X,* and *CIL XIV)*.

It will be observed from our tables that the inscriptional material from the Northern area is divided into fourth/fifth and sixth centuries, whereas inscriptions from the Central and Southern areas cover three periods, third/fourth, fifth, and sixth/seventh centuries.

In the Northern area, we do not have any specifically dated inscriptions before the fifth century, but we included here about 70 inscriptions from the military cemetery at *Concordia*. These are said to date back to the end of the fourth and the first half

INTRODUCTION   25

of the fifth centuries.[19] The few specifically dated inscriptions from this area go back to the fifth century.

In the Central area, we did not find any specifically dated inscriptions from the St. Catherine cemetery at *Clusim* (the modern Chiusi). These are said to date back to the third century.[20] Our third/fourth-century inscriptional material from this area also includes nine epitaphs from the St. Mustiola cemetery at the same location, dating back to the fourth century. Inscriptions from the seventh century total about half a dozen.

In the Southern area, we found one dated inscription from the third century. As in the Central Italian area, there are about half a dozen inscriptions from the seventh century.

H. *Rome (CIL VI)*. The supply of inscriptional material from this area alone would seem to justify its separate treatment. We limited ourselves to a total of 1,000 inscriptions, 269 of which are dated. The third and fourth centuries are treated as one group, since only 20 inscriptions were found in the former. The sixth and seventh centuries are also taken together, since we found only three inscriptions attributed to the latter century.

5. METHOD OF ANALYSIS

The method used to analyze the data from the inscriptions is the same as that used by P. Gaeng and S. W. Omeltchenko. A count is made of all occurrences of the expected *B* and *V* spelling and deviations therefrom in interior (intervocalic and postconsonantal) and initial positions in both dated and undated inscriptions. The extent of deviation is then compared among the various areas, together with percentage figures, whenever the number of examples seems to justify such a procedure.

A matter which has implications for this entire study is when to regard deviations from traditional orthography as random mistakes and when to regard them as indications of possible phono-

---

[19] August Friedrich von Pauly, *Paulys Real-Encyclopädie der Altertumwissenschaft*, Band IV (Stuttgart: J. B. Metzier, 1901), p. 831.
[20] *Ibid.*, p. 118.

logical change. In order to guide our reactions to particular percentage figures in the various areas, we have established, on the basis of internal evidence from the inscriptions, a control figure of five percent. Deviations of less than five percent will be interpreted as random mistakes, and deviations amounting to more than five percent will be interpreted as indications of possible phonological change.[21] This five percent figure, which is applicable only to the present study, was arrived at in the following manner: A search of our inscriptional material from the various areas revealed that the only area which permitted us to arrive at a control figure was Africa. Here, the spellings *D* and *P* for an expected *V* are the most obvious examples we have of orthographic errors. In the third person singular perfect tense ending of REQUIESCERE and of other verbs, we found thirty-five cases of the expected *V* spelling and one deviation each with *D* and *P*. Taken together we get a 5.4 % figure. We chose the nearest whole percent.

The *B* and *V* spellings in verb endings were examined separately and were found to be of no major importance to grammar. Seeing that here the *B* and *V* are actually in intervocalic position, data concerning these two spellings in verb endings are taken together with other data concerning the *B* and *V* in interior position (intervocalic and postconsonantal) in the section designated *SUMMARY: the Latin /b/ and /u̯/ in Interior Position,* which appears at the end of each chapter of the various areas. Once it can be determined that the percentage figures showing deviations represent a phonologically established phenomenon, we then proceed to make general statements regarding a possible chronology on the basis of dated inscriptions in our corpus.

In the case of a language like Latin, of course, our data here consist not of sounds heard, but of letters visible, and it is on the use of the letters that the analysis is based. Our data lend themselves easily to quantitative representation, and it is by covering large amounts of data at once that much is done to persuade us that the emergence of consistent patterns of orthographic deviations from the norm are not just accidental, random phenomena.

---

[21] A similar procedure was used by Robert D. King in an article entitled "Weakly Stressed Vowels in Old Saxon," *Word,* XXI, No. 1, April, 1965.

An attempt has been made to exhaust the data from our corpus, to evaluate every item for its validity (since mere numbers may sometimes be misleading),[22] and to give qualitative statements concerning the phenomenon in question.

We have confronted our task in three steps: (1) in order to keep evidence of inscriptions distinct from information about Vulgar Latin obtained from other sources and to draw conclusions from percentage figures based on internal evidence from the inscriptions alone, we have established a control figure to separate deviations which are to be taken as random mistakes from those which are to be taken as indications of phonological change; (2) in order to reduce the margin of error in interpreting our data, we have referred to other studies of documentary materials which have given some consideration to the phenomenon in question, and have integrated the results of such studies into our own quantitative-comparative analysis; (3) we have checked the evolution of the Latin /b/ and /u̯/ and its distribution in late Latin speech as recoverable through quantitative techniques against its distribution in existing Romance languages and dialects in their immediately accessible spoken forms; similarities and differences in the evolution of these two consonants in late Latin and Romance are pointed out.

6. The *B* and *V* Spelling in Latin Inscriptions

The basic problem that confronts us in our study of the inscriptions is consistency or lack of consistency in the use of the expected *B* and *V* spellings, and how we are going to interpret it. Consistency in the use of the expected *B* and *V* spellings (measured in terms of deviations amounting to less than five percent) in a given position is taken as evidence that the phonemic distinction between the original Latin /b/ and /u̯/ was preserved.

---

[22] A particular instance of this concerns deviations found in proper nouns. Proper nouns alone, we believe, are not sufficient evidence of a Vulgar phenomenon supposed to have been common. Here, deviations may be due to a possible lack of a strong orthographic tradition. As a result, throughout the present study, we have corrected our figures on the basis of deviations not including proper nouns.

Deviations in a given position amounting to more than five percent are taken as evidence that the originally distinct Latin /b/ and /u̯/ were no longer phonemically distinct in that position. To describe this phenomenon the term *merger* will be used. This term is, in itself, a neutral term with respect to phonetic-phonemic result.

Yet, it may be possible to observe a *B-V* alternation in the inscriptions from a particular area where deviations from the expected spelling in a given position are skewed, i.e., we find a predominance of *B* spellings for the expected *V*, or conversely a predominance of *V* spellings for the expected *B*. Both kinds of spellings are evidence of one and the same phenomenon, namely a merger in that position of the originally distinct Latin /b/ and /u̯/. In such a case, it is the skewing in favor of one or the other deviant graphemes which requires explanation, not the expected *B-V* alternation resulting from a Latin /b/-/u̯/ merger.

In a given region, consistent skewings in favor of *B* spellings for *V*, although good evidence of a merger, may be due to more than a chance distribution and may reflect, as suggested by P. Gaeng (p. 100, note 64) "a spirantization of the labio-velar phoneme," i.e., strengthening of the articulation of the /u̯/, making it a true bilabial fricative, which perhaps may have been identified in some way with the original Latin /b/.

On the other hand, in a given region, a predominance of *V* spellings for the expected *B*, although good evidence of a merger, would seem to point to an orthographic practice on the part of stonemasons from that region of spelling what they heard, i.e., the fricative that they heard in a position where the original Latin /b/ and /u̯/ remained phonemically distinct as an occlusive and a fricative.[23] A possible structural explanation may also be considered to account for the less frequent use of *B* for original /u̯/ (*infra*, Part II, Sec. 12, Lugdunensis; Sec. 13, Northern Italy).

---

[23] There is a basic problem of what kind of training the stone-masons may have had. They may have been taught the phonetic values of an alphabet (as we might learn the IPA) and gone out and wrote down the pronunciation as they heard it. Here there arises a problem of fit between the values of the alphabet and the values of the actual pronunciation. On the other hand, they may have been taught the received spelling of certain words — even in large number — and extrapolated from there the spelling of words they had not been actually taught.

How do we interpret a *B-V* alternation in a position where no merger has caused it? It may not be unreasonable to think that stonemasons, somewhat uncertain of the use of the two letters in a position where a merger has taken place, also misused the *B* and *V* spellings in other positions, where it would otherwise have been easy to remember the traditional spelling because of a conservation of a sound (phonemic) distinction in that position.

Finally, we must keep in mind the possibility that in a given area a strong orthographic tradition may conceal linguistic change, and so the language may continue to be represented as though it had not changed. English and French, with their largely medieval orthography, are examples of this. For example, French *eau* is pronounced /o/ in the modern language, and English *light* is pronunced /lajt/ in the modern language, but both spellings reflect a former state.

We may now begin our investigation of the *B-V* alternation in Latin Inscriptions.

Part II

THE *B-V* ALTERNATION IN LATIN INSCRIPTIONS: AREAS

7. BRITAIN

1. *Intervocalic Position*

1.1 CLat. *B* /b/

Area	Century	(B) → B	(B) → V
Britain (Pagan)	I	4	0
	II	6	0
	III	30	1
	IV	9	0
	n. d.	46	0
	Totals	95	1
Britain (Christ.)	IV	0	0
	V	1	0
	VI	6	0
	VII	0	0
	VIII/IX	2	0
	n. d.	2	0
	Totals	11	0

(a) *Britain (Pagan)*. Among all our dated and undated pagan Roman inscriptions from Britain, we found only a single instance in which Latin intervocalic /b/ was spelled with the letter *V*. This occurs in a nominative singular form VIVIUS (*Coll.* 17), for the proper noun VIBIUS, in a third century inscription from London. There are a total of 95 correct spellings for this consonant and in another five occurrences, VIBIANUS (*Coll.* 2042 a. 253), VIBIA (*Coll.* 165, no date), VIBI (*Coll.* 475, no date), VIBIUS (*Coll.* 508, no date), and VIBIUS (*Coll.* 1327, no date), this proper noun appears correctly spelled in our inscriptional material from this area.

It is also worth noting that this *V* spelling for intervocalic *B* is limited to a proper noun; consequently, its validity as evidence of a possible *B-V* alternation in Britain may be questioned on the grounds of a possible lack of orthographic tradition, which would increase the likelihood of misspelling, just as we are likely to misspell a proper noun with whose spelling we are not familiar. Hence, we believe this single deviation is of doubtful significance. It appears that Collingwood's observation of this form is too general: "VIVIUS, a variant of VIBIUS. This substitution of letters occurs even in later inscriptions."[1]

(b) *Britain (Christ.).* In our Christian Latin inscriptions from Britain, we did not find a single example of *V* for *B* in intervocalic position.

1.2   CLat. *V* /u̯/

Area	Century	(V) → V	(V) → B
Britain (Pagan)	I	12	0
	II	18	0
	III	15	0
	IV	18	0
	n. d.	56	0
	Totals	119	0
Britain (Christ.)	IV	1	0
	V	5	0
	VI	6	0
	VII	0	0
	VIII/IX	2	0
	n. d.	6	0
	Totals	20	0

(a) *Britain (Pagan).* In our entire corpus of pagan inscriptions from this area, we found no examples of *B* for *V* in intervocalic position.

---

[1] R. G. Collingwood and R. P. Wright, *The Roman Inscriptions of Britain* (Oxford: Clarendon Press, 1965), p. 9.

32 THE EVOLUTION OF THE LATIN /b/ - /u̯/ MERGER

(b) *Britain (Christ.)*. As in our pagan Roman inscriptions from Britain, Latin intervocalic /u̯/ always appears as V in orthography, in the Christian inscriptions also.

2. *Postconsonantal Position*

2.1 CLat. *B* after /l/

Area	Century	(-LB-) → -LB-	(-LB-) → -LV-
Britain (Pagan)	I	0	0
	II	1	0
	III	0	0
	IV	0	0
	n. d.	1	0
	Totals	2	0
Britain (Christ.)	IV	0	0
	V	0	0
	VI	0	0
	VII	0	0
	VIII/IX	0	0
	n. d.	0	0
	Totals	0	0

(a) *Britain (Pagan)*. There are only two occurrences of words with -LB- and no deviations.

(b) *Britain (Christ.)*. In Christian Latin inscriptions from Britain, words with -LB- do not occur.

2.2 CLat. *B* after /r/

Area	Century	(-RB-) → -RB-	(-RB-) → -RV-
Britain (Pagan)	I	0	0
	II	2	0
	III	0	0
	IV	0	0
	n. d.	3	0
	Totals	5	0
Britain (Christ.)	IV	0	0
	V	0	0
	VI	0	0
	VII	0	0
	VIII/IX	0	0
	n. d.	0	0
	Totals	0	0

THE *B-V* ALTERNATION IN LATIN INSCRIPTIONS 33

(a) *Britain (Pagan)*. There are only five occurrences of words with the expected *-RB-* spelling and no deviations in our corpus of pagan Roman inscriptions from Britain.

(b) *Britain (Christ.)*. In Christian Roman inscriptions from Britain, words with *-RB-* do not occur.

2.3 CLat. *V* after /l/

Area	Century	(-LV-) → -LV-	(-LV-) → -LB-
Britain (Pagan)	I	0	0
	II	9	0
	III	4	0
	IV	0	0
	n. d.	13	0
	Total	26	0
Britain (Christ.)	IV	0	0
	V	0	0
	VI	1	0
	VII	0	0
	VIII/IX	0	0
	n. d.	0	0
	Total	1	0

(a) *Britain (Pagan)*. There are twenty-six occurrences of the expected *-LV-* spelling in pagan inscriptions from this area and no deviations.

(b) *Britain (Christ.)*. There is only one occurrence of the expected *-LV-* spelling in Christian inscriptions from Britain and no deviations.

2.4 CLat. *V* after /r/

Area	Century	(-RV-) → -RV-	(-RV-) → -RB-
Britain (Pagan)	I	1	0
	II	2	0
	III	0	0
	IV	0	0
	n. d.	9	0
	Total	12	0

34   THE EVOLUTION OF THE LATIN /b/ - /u̯/ MERGER

Area	Century	(-RV-)→-RV-	(-RV-)→-RB-
Britain (Christ.)	IV	0	0
	V	0	0
	VI	1	0
	VII	0	0
	VIII/IX	0	0
	n. d.	0	0
	Total	1	0

(a) *Britain (Pagan)*. There are twelve occurrences of words with the expected *-RV-* spelling and no deviations with *-RB-*.

(b) *Britain (Christ.)* There is only one occurrence of the expected *-RV-* spelling and no deviation with *-RB-*.

In Britain, the Latin /b/ and /u̯/ remained distinct in post-consonantal position.

3. CLat. V /u̯/ *in perfect tense endings of REQUIE-VIT and of other verbs*

Area	Century	(-VIT)→-VIT	(-VIT)→-BIT	%
Britain (Pagan)	I	2	0	
	II	2	0	
	III	7	0	
	IV	0	0	
	n. d.	12	0	
	Totals	23	0	
Britain (Christ.)	IV	1	0	
	V	1	0	
	VI	0	0	
	VII	0	0	
	VIII/IX	2	2	50.0
	n. d.	2	0	
	Totals	6	2	25.0

(a) *Britain (Pagan)*. There are twenty-three occurrences of the expected *-VIT* ending in pagan Roman inscriptions from Britain. We found no examples of *B* for *V* in this tense ending. We found two occurrences (not included in our table here, but included in our total count) of the third person plural perfect active indicative ending *-VERUNT,* both correctly spelled.

(b) *Britain (Christ.).* In our eighth/ninth-century Christian Latin inscriptions from Britain,[2] we found two examples of a confusion between *B* and *V* in this perfect tense ending. These occur in the forms PROPE[RA]BIT (= PRAEPARAVIT) (*Coll.* 1011, ca. 870) and PROBARABIT (= PRAEPARAVIT) (*Coll.* 1015, ca. VIII/IX cent.). The dating of these forms is very late and beyond the chronological limits that are pertinent to a study of Vulgar Latin inscriptions. It is also worth noting that the *-VIT* ending occurs quite infrequently (a total of six times) in our Christian Latin inscriptions from Britain (partially due to the fact that the consecrated expression is HIC IACET), so that the 25 % over-all figure would not, of course, represent the state of affairs. With these considerations in mind, we could hardly cite these two deviations as evidence of a possible merger of Latin /b/ and /u̯/ in the intervocalic position in the Vulgar Latin of Christian Britain. There were no occurrences of other perfect tense endings.

4. *Initial Position*

4.1 CLat. *B* /b/

Area	Century	(B) → B	(B) → V
Britain (Pagan)	I	4	0
	II	9	0
	III	18	0
	IV	2	0
	n. d.	38	0
	Total	71	0
Britain (Christ.)	IV	0	0
	V	1	0
	VI	6	0
	VII	1	0
	VIII/IX	0	0
	n. d.	1	0
	Total	9	0

(a) *Britain (Pagan).* There are a total of seventy-one occurrences of the expected *B* spelling in initial position and no deviations.

---

[2] It is doubtful that Latin was a vernacular in Britain at this time.

(b) *Britain (Christ.)*. There were a total of nine occurrences of the expected initial *B* spelling and no deviations.

4.2 CLat. *V* /u̯/

Area	Century	(V) → V	(V) → B
Britain (Pagan)	I	16	0
	II	53	0
	III	55	0
	IV	16	0
	n. d.	198	2
	Total	338	2
Britain (Christ.)	IV	1	0
	V	4	0
	VI	8	0
	VII	1	0
	VIII/IX	0	0
	n. d.	2	0
	Total	16	0

(a) *Britain (Pagan)*. Among all our pagan Roman inscriptions from Britain, we found only two examples of an initial *B-V* confusion, and these in a single undated inscription which reads HOMINIBUS BAGIS BITAM for HOMINIBUS VAGIS VITAM (*Coll.* 1). Since the two *B* spellings for the expected initial *V* spelling were found on the same inscription, they may represent the errors of a single individual only. Thus, these two forms need not be taken as evidence of a possible confusion between /b/ and /u̯/ in Britain.

(b) *Britain (Christ.)*. There were a total of sixteen occurrences of the expected initial *V* spelling and no deviations in either dated or undated Christian Roman inscriptions from Britain.

5. *Summary and Conclusions*

We may now attempt to summarize our data concerning the use of *B* and *V* to represent the Latin /b/ and /u̯/ in the Roman inscriptions from Britain.

5.1 SUMMARY: *The Latin /b/ and /u̯/ in the Interior Position*

Our corpus of Latin inscriptions from Britain, which extend from the first century A. D. well into the Vulgar Latin period show an absence of any reliable orthographic indication of a possible Latin intervocalic /b/ - /u̯/ merger. There were a total of 113 occurrences of the expected interior *B* spelling and only one deviation (or 0.9 %) with *V*. This is found in a proper noun and is of doubtful significance.

There are only two examples of the use of *B* for *V* in this position. These occur in the third person singular perfect active indicative of PRAEPARARE, and, they too, are of doubtful significance, because they are of a rather late date (eighth/ninth century). On the basis of 208 occurrences of the expected interior *V* and only two deviations (or 0.9 %) with *B*, we would be justified in stating that the Latin interior /b/ was quite stable in Britain. Evidence of stability of the interior *B* and of the interior *V* means an absence of a merger of the two Latin consonants represented by these letters.

5.2 SUMMARY: *The Latin /b/ and /u̯/ in the Initial Position*

Data concerning the use of the *B* and *V* spellings in initial position reveal that we actually have only one reliable example of an initial *B-V* confusion in the forms BAGIS BITAM. Since both forms are found on the same inscription, they are treated as a single deviation. On the basis of a total of eighty occurrences of the expected initial *B* spelling and no deviations with *V*, and a total of 354 occurrences of the expected initial *V* spelling from both pagan and Christian inscriptions and only one deviation, we may assume that the Latin initial /b/ and /u̯/ were quite stable in Britain. In his study of the *B-V* alternation in inscriptions from the Vulgar Latin period, Parodi (*op. cit.*, pp. 181-182, note 1) makes no mention of any apparent confusion in the use of these two letters in this area; in fact, he expressly states that "i *v* e i *b* sono in tutti perfetta regola."

What is striking in our investigation of the *B* and *V* in the Latin inscriptions from Britain is the paucity of reliable evidence of an identification of Latin intervocalic /b/ with /u̯/, because this change took place in the Latin of the greater Empire. There is not a single conclusive example of *V* for *B* or of the reverse phenomenon in our source books, *Roman Inscriptions of Britain*, edited by Collingwood, a collection of 2,314 pagan inscriptions, and 77 Christian inscriptions from the *Corpus Inscriptiones Insularum Celticarum*, edited by Macalister.

The results of our own investigation find support in the writing of the British scholar Robert Jackson, who, in *Language and History of Early Britain*[3] writes the following regarding the Latin /b/ and /u̯/ in Britain:

> Latin *v* and intervocalic *b* remained rigidly distinct in British, clearly because they were pronounced in British /u̯/ and /b/ respectively. It is significant that neither in the Latin inscriptions of Roman Britain nor in the later inscriptions of the Dark Ages ... are there any examples of confusion of *v* and *b*.... We can be reasonably sure, then, that *v* and intervocalic *b* retained their earlier values in British Latin; and it is to be noted that this seems to agree with the pronunciation of the more educated among the Continental speakers of Vulgar Latin by contrast with that or the mass of the population.

That the Latin /b/ and /u̯/ remained distinct in Britain is also evidenced by the fact that Latin loan words into English show an absence of any modification of the Latin /b/ and /u̯/. Concerning the nature of these loan words, Jackson (*op. cit.*, p. 80) writes: "These [loan words] are for the most part not "learned" loans from book Latin and written sources, but popular borrowings from the living Latin tongue in Roman Britain."

5.3 Conclusions

S. W. Omeltchenko (*op. cit.*, p. 567) sums up his conclusions concerning the vocalism of the Latin spoken in Britain and North Africa when he writes: "Although both areas follow classical orthography almost scrupulously, the Latin of Britain maintains its purity even more so than that of Africa, a linguistic reality

---

[3] Robert Jackson, *Language and History of Early Britain* (Edinberg: Edinberg University Press, 1953), pp. 89-90.

THE *B-V* ALTERNATION IN LATIN INSCRIPTIONS 39

which has been repeatedly observed in this work." From the point of view of dialectal differences, Omeltchenko's conclusions concerning the preservation of Latin vocalic features in Britain and our conclusions regarding the preservation of the distinction between Latin /b/ and /u̯/ are important phonological features which distinguish the Latin spoken in Britain from the Latin spoken throughout the greater Empire. Percentage figures based on data found in pagan inscriptions alone show the preservation of Latin /b/ and /u̯/ in all positions, as do percentage figures based on data from Christian inscriptions alone. We conclude, therefore, that the inclusion of pagan inscriptions from Britain has had no effect on our findings.

8. THE BALKANS

1. *Intervocalic Position*

1.1 CLat. B /b/

Area	Century	(B) → B	(B) → V	%
Balkans (Pagan)	I	2	0	
	II	4	0	
	III	2	1	
	IV	3	0	
	n. d.	17	1	
	Totals	28	2	6.6
Balkans (Christ.)	IV	6	0	
	V	0	0	
	VI	0	0	
	n. d.	14	0	
	Totals	20	0	

(a) *Balkans (Pagan)*. With the exception of two forms, Latin intervocalic /b/ appears as *B* in the pagan Roman inscriptions from the Balkans. Following are the examples of deviations, from the third century:

LIVES (= LIBENS) (Kalinka 125 a. 246/247)

In an undated inscription we found one instance where intervocalic /b/ is represented by *V*. This occurs in the form:

HAVETIS (= HABETIS) (Kalinka 379)

(b) *Balkans (Christ.)*. In our Christian inscriptions from the Balkans, Latin intervocalic /b/ always appears written with a *B*. The Latin /b/ appears once with the expected *B* spelling in the future tense ending *-BIT* in undated inscriptions.

1.2 CLat. V'/u̯/

Area	Century	(V) → V	(V) → B
Balkans (Pagan)	I	3	0
	II	5	0
	III	8	0
	IV	0	0
	n. d.	15	0
	Totals	31	0
Balkans (Christ.)	IV	2	0
	V	0	0
	VI	0	0
	n. d.	18	0
	Totals	20	0

In our entire corpus of pagan and Christian Roman inscriptions from the Balkans, we found no examples of the reverse spelling, i.e., *B* for *V* in the intervocalic position. Latin intervocalic /u̯/ was quite stable in this area.

2. *Postconsonantal Position*

2.1 CLat. *B* after /l/

Area	Century	(-LB-) → -LB-	(-LB-) → -LV-
Balkans (Pagan)	I	0	0
	II	0	0
	III	0	0
	IV	0	0
	n. d.	0	0
	Totals	0	0
Balkans (Christ.)	IV	0	0
	V	0	0
	VI	0	0
	n. d.	0	0
	Totals	0	0

In our entire corpus of Latin inscriptions from the Balkans (pagan and Christian) words with -LB- do not occur.

2.2 CLat. B after /r/

Area	Century	(-RB-)→-RB-	(-RB-)→-RV-	OTHER
Balkans (Pagan)	I	0	0	
	II	0	0	
	III	0	0	
	IV	0	0	
	n. d.	0	0	1
	Totals	0	0	1
Balkans (Christ.)	IV	1	0	
	V	1	0	
	VI	0	0	
	n. d.	3	0	
	Totals	5	0	

(a) *Balkans (Pagan).* In pagan inscriptions from this area, words with -RB- do not occur. There is one instance where the expected -RB- appears as -RP-. This occurs on an undated inscription in the form SUPERPO (*Kalinka* 442) for SUPERBO. Since this is an isolated case, it is evidently due to a stonecutter's slip.

(b) *Balkans (Christ.).* As can be seen from the table, there are only a total of five occurrences of the expected -RB- spelling in Christian inscriptions from the Balkans and no deviations.

2.3 CLat V after /l/

Area	Century	(-LV-)→-LV-	(-LV-)→-LB-
Balkans (Pagan)	I	0	0
	II	0	0
	III	0	0
	IV	0	0
	n. d.	3	0
	Totals	3	0
Balkans (Christ.)	IV	0	0
	V	0	0
	VI	0	0
	n. d.	0	0
	Totals	0	0

42   THE EVOLUTION OF THE LATIN /b/ - /u̯/ MERGER

(a) *Balkans (Pagan)*. In the pagan inscriptions from this area, there are only three occurrences of words with the expected -*LV*- spelling and no deviations.

(b) *Balkans (Christ.)*. In the Christian inscriptions, words with -*LV*- do not occur.

2.4   CLat. *V* after /r/

Area	Century	(-RV-)→-RV	(-RV-)→-RB-
Balkans (Pagan)	I	1	0
	II	0	0
	III	0	0
	IV	0	0
	n. d.	1	0
	Totals	2	0
Balkans (Christ.)	IV	0	0
	V	0	0
	VI	0	0
	n. d.	1	0
	Totals	1	0

(a) *Balkans (Pagan)*. There are only two occurrences of the expected -*RV*- spelling and no deviations.

(b) *Balkans (Christ.)*. There is only one occurrence of the expected -*RV*- spelling in the Christian inscriptions and no deviation.

In our entire corpus of inscriptions from the Balkans, there are few occurrences of the expected *B* and *V* in postconsonantal position, and when they do appear, they are always correctly spelled. On the basis of such a scanty sampling, it would be difficult to make any general statement regarding the *B* and *V* in this position.

3. *CLat.* V /u̯/ *in perfect tense endings of REQUIE-VIT, and of other verbs*

The Latin *V* appears quite infrequently in the inscriptions from the Balkans. Because of the scanty sampling of this verb form and the fact that even a single deviation may give a high percentage figure that may not represent the state of affairs, we decided to omit a tabular representation and percentage figures altogether.

(a) *Balkans (Pagan)*. In our entire corpus of pagan inscriptions from the Balkans, there are no occurrences of the expected *V* in his tense ending. There is one occurrence of the expected *V* in the third person plural ending -*VERUNT*. There are no occurrences of the future tense endings.

(b) *Balkans (Christ.)*. In dated inscriptions, neither the perfect nor the future tense endings occur. In undated inscriptions, the expected *V* spelling occurs three times in the third person singular and once in the first person singular in the perfect tense. We found only one example of the use of *B* for *V*. This occurs in the form SUSCITABIT for SUSCITAVIT (*D*. 3476), no date.

Initial Position

.1 CLat. *B* /b/

Area	Century	(B) → B	(B) → V
Balkans (Pagan)	I	0	0
	II	1	0
	III	2	0
	IV	0	0
	n. d.	16	0
	Totals	19	0
Balkans (Christ.)	IV	3	1
	V	0	0
	VI	0	0
	n. d.	19	0
	Totals	22	1

(a) *Balkans (Pagan)*. There were nineteen occurrences of the expected initial *B* spelling in pagan Balkan inscriptions and no deviations.

(b) *Balkans (Christ.)*. There were a total of twenty-two occurrences of the expected initial *B* spelling in Christian inscriptions from the Balkans and one deviation with *V*. This occurs in fourth-century inscription from the region of Pannonia and reads:

VENEMERENTI (= BENEMERENTI) (*D*. 1480 a. 385)

On the basis of a total of forty-one occurrences of the expected initial *B* spelling and only a single deviation (or 2.4 %) with *V*, it is reasonable to think that the Latin initial /b/, spelled almost universally *B*, is quite stable in this area.

4.2 CLat. *V* /u̯/

Area	Century	(V) → V	(V) → B
Balkans (Pagan)	I	0	0
	II	3	0
	III	7	0
	IV	5	0
	n. d.	98	0
	Totals	113	0
Balkans (Christ.)	IV	6	0
	V	1	0
	VI	0	0
	n. d.	63	0
	Totals	70	0

(a) *Balkans (Pagan)*. There were 113 occurrences of the expected initial *V* spelling and no deviations.

(b) *Balkans (Christ.)*. In the Christian inscriptions from the Balkans, there were a total of seventy occurrences of the expected initial *V* spelling and no deviations. On the basis of a total of 183 occurrences of the expected initial *V* spelling and no deviations with *B*, we would be justified in stating that the Latin initial /u̯/ was quite stable in the Balkans.

5. *Summary and Conclusions*

We may now attempt to summarize our data concerning the *B* and the *V* spellings in the Balkans.

5.1 SUMMARY: *The Latin /b/ and /u̯/ in the Interior Position*

A review of our data concerning the use of *B* and *V* in both pagan and Christian inscriptions from the Balkans shows a paucity of evidence of a possible identification of Latin /b/ with /u̯/ in the intervocalic position. In our complete corpus of inscriptions from this area, there were a total of fifty-four occurrences of the expected interior *B* spelling and only two deviations (or 3.6 %) with *V*. There is one example of the use of *B* for *V* in a perfect tense ending, as against sixty-two cases of the interior *V*. This gives a 1.8 % figure. Since both figures are below our five percent control figure, we conclude that the Latin /b/ and /u̯/ remained distinct in the Balkan regions. That the intervocalic /b/ - /u̯/ merger[4] was a late development in the history of Roumanian seems to be evidenced by the fact that there is an absence of deviations from the expected Latin *B* and *V* spellings in Christian inscriptions which extend through the sixth century.

5.2 SUMMARY: *The Latin /b/ and /u̯/ in the Initial Position*

In the pagan and Christian inscriptions from the Balkans, which extend from the first century A. D. through the sixth century, there occur a total of forty-one occurrences of the expected initial *B* and only one deviation with *V* in a Christian inscription from the latter part of the fourth century. There occur a total of 183 occurrences of the expected initial *V* and no deviations. While there is no question that a merger of Latin initial /b/ and /u̯/ occurs in some cases in modern Roumanian as evidenced by forms like *batrîn* < VETERANUS and *berbec* < VERVECEM,[5] there is no evidence of a possible beginning of this phenomenon in the Vulgar Latin of the Danubian Provinces.

In the Balkans, as in Britain, percentage figures based on data found in pagan inscriptions alone as well as those based on data from Christian inscriptions alone show the preservation of the original Latin /b/ and /u̯/ in all positions. The inclusion of pagan inscriptions from the Balkans has, therefore, not altered our findings.

In a study of inscriptional material from the Danubian province of Pannonia,[6] the Hungarian scholar V. Luzsénszky cites only one example where Latin intervocalic /b/ was misspelled. This occurs in the proper noun FADIANO (= FABIANO), found in an in-

---

[4] Hariton Tiktin, *Rumänisches Elementarbuch* (Heidelberg: C. Winter, 1905), pp. 54-56.

[5] *Ibid.*

[6] V. Luszénszky, "A pannónai latin feliratok nyelvtana" in *Egyetemes Philologiai Közlöny*, 57 (May-July 1933), 96.

scription dated 201 A. D. Since this is an isolated case, it would seem to be due to a stonecutter's error. Luzsénszky also gives what appears to be an inappropriate example of V for B in the shortened form INV, which he attempts to clarify as IMPERATOR. He does not give quantitative data concerning the use of B and V, nor does he give other examples of an alternation in the use of these two letters.

Perhaps the most important work written in the past few decades concerned with the language of inscriptions from the Danubian provinces, and which is also a synthesis of documentary material culled from studies of other areas of the Empire, is H. Mihăescu's: *Limba latină in provinciile dunărene ale imperiului român*. The extent of Mihăescu's study is given by his own words:

> am certetet inscripțile și textele din primele șaseveracuri ale erei noastre din provincile romane Dalmația, Noricum, Pannonia superioara și inferioara, Moesia superioara și inferioara și Dacia.[7]

Mihăescu sums up his conclusions concerning the Latin of the Danubian Provinces thus:

> Faptele linguistice păstrate în înscriptiile și textele din provinciile dunărene sînt numeroase și variate, dar nu sînt nici specifice acestor ținutiri și nîci unice. Pentru fiecare din ele m-am străduit să culeg fenomene analogice din opus si arm reusit aproape pretutindeni. Aceasta înseamnă că ele erau fenomena sau inovatii raspîndite pe un spațiu mai larg. Rezultă, prin urmare, că provinciile dunărene nu formau un domeniu linguistic izolat independent.[8]

---

[7] H. Mihăescu, *Limba latină in provinciile dunărene ale imperiului român* (Bucharest: Editura Academiei Republici Romîne, 1960). The work is not based entirely on inscriptions, but the textual material must be considered secondary on the basis of the more than 21,000 inscriptions that were studied. Translation of the Rumanian: "I have investigated the inscriptions and texts of the first six centuries of our era of the Roman provinces of Dalmatia, Noricum, Pannonia Superior and Inferior, Moesia Superior and Inferior, and Dacia," p. 5.

[8] Translation of the Rumanian: "The linguistic facts preserved in inscriptions and texts from the Danubian provinces are numerous and varied, but they are neither peculiar to these areas nor unique. For each

Mihăescu's important conclusion that the Latin of the Danubian provinces shows an absence of distinctive dialectical traits is based on the assumption that deviations from the norm are neither specific nor unique to this area, but are found in most of the Empire, and thus it appears that the inscriptions show that the Latin of this area was evolving in the same way as that of other areas.

Although this conclusion has for the most part been accepted by some scholars,[9] others have questioned it on the grounds that he has not given quantitative data showing the frequency of occurrence of expected forms and deviations therefrom. G. Messing[10] remarks that "if one were to reason from the frequency of forms in the Danube provinces of their absence, one might reach conclusions decidedly at variance with Mihăescu's." S. Stati[11] points out the absence of quantitative and comparative data concerning noun and verb endings. G. Straka[12] believes that "quand on aura rendu la valeur exacte aux graphies relevées, ces différences apparaîtront tout de même plus grandes que l'auteur ne semble vouloir admettre."

Mihăescu (Secs. 77-78) believes that an intervocalic /b/ - /u̯/ merger existed in the Danubian provinces as it did in most other areas of the Empire. This conclusion seems to obtain for the Latin of Dalmatia only (*infra*, Part II, Sec. 9), although it must be kept in mind that for this area Mihăescu's conclusion was not reached

---

of them I have endeavored to collect similar phenomena from the West and I have succeeded in almost every case. This means that they were phenomena or innovations spread over a wider area. It follows that the Danubian provinces did not form an isolated or independent linguistic zone."

[9] Rudolf Hanslik, in his review of Mihăescu's work in *Kratylos*, 10 (1965) says (p. 213) that "Die Schlussfolgerung von M[ihăescu] aus dem Gesamtmaterial ist absolut richtig." Väänänen in his review in *Neuphilologische Mitteilungen*, LXII (1961), 228, likewise concurs. G. Straka states in his review, *Revue de Linguistique Romane*, XXIV (1960), p. 404, that "l'auteur en conclut avec raison, qu'il n'y avait pas de différences sensibles entre le latin des Balkans et celui des autres régions de l'Empire."

[10] Gordon M. Messing, *Language*, 39 (1963), 675.

[11] S. Stati, Review of *Limba latină in provinciile dunărene ale imperiului român*, by H. Mihăescu, *Studii şi Cercetari Lingvistice*, 4 (1960), 959.

[12] G. Straka, Review of *Limba latină in provinciile dunărene ale imperiului român*, by H. Mihăescu, *Revue de linguistique romane*, XXIV (1960), 404.

on the basis of a quantitative-comparative analysis. A review of his data showing an inconsistency in the use of B and V reveals that he found twelve examples of V spelling for B (three of which are in proper nouns) and nineteen examples of B spelling for V (six of which are in proper nouns). He does not give the number of forms with the expected B and V spellings. In the following tables I have assembled the data given by Mihăescu (Secs. 77-78) showing the number of deviations from the expected B and V spellings in the Roman provinces in the inner Balkan region:

(a) CLat. B /b/

Area	Interv. $(B) \to V$	Postcon. $(B) \to V$	Verb. End. $(B) \to V$	Init. $(B) \to V$	Tot. Dev. $(B) \to V$
Noricum	0	0	0	0	0
Pannonia	3	0	0	0	3
Moesia Sup.	2	0	0	0	2
Moesia Inf.	4	0	0	0	4
Dacia	(3) *	0	0	0	(3) *
Totals	12 (9)	0	0	0	12 (9)

(b) CLat. V /u̯/

Area	Interv. $(V) \to B$	Postcon. $(V) \to B$	Verb. End. $(V) \to B$	Init. $(V) \to B$	Tot. Dev. $(V) \to B$
Noricum	2	0	0	0	2
Pannonia	0	(2) *	1	0	3 (2) *
Moesia Sup.	2 (1) *	(1) *	1	0	4 (2) *
Moesia Inf.	3	0	0	4 (1) *	7 (1) *
Dacia	(1) *	0	0	2	3 (1) *
Totals	8 (6)	(3) (0)	2	6 (5)	19 (13)

An examination of the above tables shows that data concerning an inconsistency in the use of B and V in the individual provinces are meager (although it appears that the highest number of deviations from the expected B and V occurs in Moesia Inferior).

( ) * This figure represents the number of deviations in proper nouns; for example, in Dacia, 3 out 3 examples of V for intervocalic B are found in proper nouns.

( ) This figure represents the total number of reliable deviations, i.e., the total number of deviations not including proper nouns.

We have no way of knowing whether the inconsistency in the use of B an V in these provinces points to even an incipient intervocalic /b/ - /u̯/ merger, since the number of cases of the expected B and V and the percentage of deviation therefrom are not given for each province. We believe that Mihăescu's conclusion concerning the existence of an intervocalic /b/ - /u̯/ merger in these Roman provinces, reached without giving quantitative and comparative data, and without considering the reliability of some deviations (viz. those in proper nouns), may not be altogether accurate.

Our own analysis showing quantitative-comparative data concerning the use of B and V based on total occurrences of the expected spellings and deviations therefrom in the Balkans indicates that the Latin /b/ and /u̯/ were quite stable in this area during the period covered by our inscriptions and did not participate in an intervocalic merger which was prevalent in other areas of the Empire. Evidence of distinctive behavior of the /b/ and the /u̯/ leads us to conclude that a regional isogloss can be drawn for this feature of the Latin of the inner Balkans.

5.3 Conclusions

1. Evidence of stability of the Latin /b/ and of the /u̯/ in all positions means an absence of a merger of the two, i.e., the conservation of the phonemic distinction.

2. An identification of /b/ with /u̯/ in the intervocalic position, and in the initial position in some cases, appears to be a late phenomenon in the history of Roumanian.

3. With Britain, the Balkan region establishes a regional differentiation with regard to a late preservation of the distinction between Latin /b/ and /u̯/.

4. There is no evidence of a loss of Latin intervocalic /b/ in the inscriptions from the Balkan region.

50 THE EVOLUTION OF THE LATIN /b/ - /u̯/ MERGER

9. DALMATIA

1. *Intervocalic Position*

1.1 CLat. B /b/

Area	Century	(B) → B	(B) → V	%
Dalmatia	IV	5	0	
	V	3	0	
	VI	2	0	
	n. d.	61	2	1.6
	Totals	71	2	2.7

In Dalmatia, Latin intervocalic /b/ is represented by V twice in undated inscriptions only. The examples are:

IACOVUS (*D.* 2436)
EUFEVIE (= EUSEBIAE) (*D.* 3402c)

Since the two deviations occur in proper nouns (where orthographic tradition may have been lacking), there would be some doubt as to whether we can cite them as evidence of a possible Latin intervocalic /b/ - /u̯/ merger in this area. In undated inscriptions only, there are two cases of the intervocalic /b/ (B) in the future tense ending *-BIT*, and one deviation in DAVIT (= DABIT) (*D.* 507). (These latter figures are counted in our totals, not here.)

1.2 CLat. V /u̯/

Century	(V) → V	(V) → B	%
IV	4	1	(20.0)
V	9	0	
VI	1	1	(50.0)
n. d.	45	5	8.2
Totals	59	7	10.6

Examples of *B* spellings to represent Latin intervocalic /u̯/ are, from dated inscriptions:

VIBI (*D.* 1223 a. 358)
FLABBIUS (*D.* 3791A VI cent.)

in undated inscriptions:

>   V[I]BUS (= VIVOS) (D. 851)
>   VIBI and HABE (= 2nd person singular imperative AVE),
>   both on the same inscription (D. 4318A)
>   BREBIS (= BREVIS) (D. 3363)
>   CONBIBES (= CONVIVIS) (D. 835)

The 10.6 % figure based on fifty-nine occurrences of the expected V spelling and seven deviations with B is evidence of a Latin intervocalic /b/ - /u̯/ merger.

2. Postconsonantal Position

2.1 CLat. B after /l/.

Century	(-RB-) → -RB-	(-LB-) → -LV-
IV	0	0
V	0	0
VI	0	0
n. d.	0	0
Totals	0	0

In the inscriptions from Dalmatia, words with the expected -LB- do not occur.

2.2 CLat. B after /r/

Century	(-LB-) → -LB-	(-RB-) → -RV-
IV	0	0
V	0	0
VI	0	0
n. d.	3	1
Totals	3	1

As can be seen from the table, there are only three cases of the expected -RB- spelling and only one deviation with -RV- in an undated inscription. This occurs in the spelling of the place name URVECE (= URBECAE?) (D. 941). This example is of doubtful significance because of a possible lack of orthographic tradition.

2.3 CLat. V after /l/

Area	Century	(-LV-) → -LV-	(-LV-) → -LB-
Dalmatia	IV	0	0
	V	1	0
	VI	0	0
	n. d.	6	0
	Totals	7	0

There were seven occurrences of words with -LV- and no deviations.

2.4 CLat. V after /r/

Century	(-RV-) → -RV-	(-RV-) → -RB-
IV	2	0
V	0	0
VI	1	0
n. d.	4	1
Totals	7	1

Although we did not find any examples of -LB- for -LV-, we did find one example of the use of -RB- for -RV-. This occurs in an undated inscription in the form SERBI (D. 1937). We also found one example where the expected -NV- (/nu̯/) appears spelled -NB-. This occurs in an undated inscription in the form CONBIBES (= CONVIVIS) (D. 835). Words with the expected -NV- do not occur. The fourteen cases of the expected V spelling and only two deviations (or 12.5 %) with B is too small a sampling, it would seem, to permit us to draw any affirmative conclusion concerning the possibility of a postconsonantal /b/ - /u̯/ merger in this area.

3. CLat. V /u̯/ in perfect tense endings of REQUIE-VIT → REQUIE-BIT, and of other verbs in the perfect tense

Century	(-VIT) → -VIT	(-VIT) → -BIT	%
IV	0	1	
V	2	2	
VI	2	1	
n. d.	9	1	
Totals	13	5	23.5

the use of *B* for *V* in this tense ending occurs in the following forms, from the fourth century:

COLLOCABI (= COLLOCAVIT) (*D*. 3835 C a. 382)

from the fifth century:

CUNPARABID (= COMPARAVIT) and CO[N]IURABIT (*D*. 382)

The latter two forms are found on one and the same inscription. As with all cases of single deviations, they may represent the errors of a single stonemason. The only deviation found in sixth-century inscriptions occurs in the form CONPARABIT (= COMPARAVIT) (*D*. 3854).

Except for the form REQUIEBIT (*D*. 827), the Latin /u̯/ in this tense ending appears with the expected *V* in all undated inscriptions from this area. Not included in our table (but included in our total count, see Sec. 5) are one occurrence of the expected *V* in the first person plural ending -*VIMUS*, three in the third person plural ending -*VERUNT*, and one in the third person plural subjunctive ending -*VERINT*.

The five *B* spellings for *V* in the third person singular of the perfect tense and the single example of *V* for *B* in the third person singular of the future indicative are evidence of a merger in the intervocalic position of the two Latin consonants represented by these letters.

4. *Initial Position*

4.1. CLat. *B* /b/

Area	Century	(B) → B	(B) → V	%
Dalmatia	IV	2	1	
	V	5	0	
	VI	0	0	
	n. d.	31	1	
	Totals	38	2	5.0

In the inscriptions from Dalmatia, we found only two examples of *V* for initial *B*, and one of these occurs in a proper noun. The examples are, from the fourth century:

VONOSO (= BONOSO) (*D*. 3042 a. 344)

In an undated inscription, we found one example of the use of *V* for initial *B* in the expression VISSENOS... ANNIS (*D*. 4735) for an expected BISSENOS (twice six), where the cardinal and distributive numerals appear written as one word. The Latin initial /b/, written almost universally *B*, seems stable in the Latin of Dalmatia.

4.2. CLat. V /u̯/

Area	Century	(V) → V	(V) → B	%
Dalmatia	IV	18	0	0.0
	V	22	2	8.3
	VI	3	1	(25.0)
	n. d.	126	5	4.0
	Totals	169	8	4.7

There were eight occurrences of the use of *B* for initial *V* in the inscriptions from Dalmatia. Following are deviations found in dated inscriptions:

BALENTES (= VALENTIS) (*D*. 3870 a. 426)
BIRGINIAM (= VIRGINIAM) (*D*. 838 V cent.)
BIXIT (= VIXIT) (*D*. 1653 VI cent.)

The 25 % figure in sixth-century inscriptions may not represent the state of affairs, since there were only three occurrences of the expected classical *V* spelling and only one deviation with *B*. In undated inscriptions we found the following forms in which the Latin initial /u̯/ was represented with the letter *B*.

BYRGO (= VIRGO) (*D*. 2934)
BIXIT (*D*. 3835)
BELIS (= 2nd person singular, present subjunctive of VELLERE)
BAL. and BALERIANO, on the same inscription (*D*. 675N)

5. *Summary and Conclusions*

We may now attempt to summarize our data concerning the use of *B* and *V* in the inscriptions from Dalmatia to see if they give us any indication of a possible Latin intervocalic /b/ - /u̯/ merger. Our criteria in this connection will be the total correct occurrences of *B* and *V* and the percentage of deviation therefrom. To the extent that we are able, we will also attempt to establish a possible chronology of intervocalic /b/ - /u̯/ merger in this area.

5.1. SUMMARY: *The Latin /b/ and /u̯/ in the Interior Position*

Data concerning the use of *V* for interior *B* do not give us adequate evidence of a possible Latin intervocalic /b/ - /u̯/ merger. There were a total of 76 occurrences of the expected interior *B* spelling and four deviations (or 5.0 %) with *V*. This figure alone may be misleading, since it includes three deviations, i.e., three *V* spellings for *B* in proper nouns. These are of doubtful significance. If we leave these items out of our count, we get a 1.4 % figure based on only one reliable deviation in the verb form DAVIT for DABIT. This alone is insufficient evidence of a Latin intervocalic /b/ - /u̯/ merger.

On the other hand, reverse spellings, i.e., *B* for interior *V* occur with a somewhat more reliability and consistency. There were a total of 91 occurrences of the expected interior *V* spelling and fourteen deviations (or 13.3 %) with *B*. This is substantial evidence, we believe, to indicate an intervocalic /b/ - /u̯/ merger in the Vulgar Latin of Dalmatia. This would be in agreement with the conclusion reached by P. Skok,[13] who also found evidence of an intervocalic /b/ - /u̯/ merger in this area. His conclusion, however, is not based on a quantitative-comparative analysis of data.

5.2. SUMMARY: *The Latin /b/ and /u̯/ in the Initial Position*

In initial position, both figures showing a *B-V* alternation are borderline cases (exactly 5 % for the expected initial *B* on the basis of only two deviations, as against thirty-eight correct spellings, one in a proper noun). This could reduce the figure to 2.5 %. The 4.7 % *B* for the expected initial *V* spelling is based on eight deviations as against 169 correct classical spellings, two of which are found in proper nouns on one and the same inscription. This

---

[13] Peta Skok, *Pojave vulgarno-latinskoga jezika na natpisima rimske provincije Dalmacije*, pp. 50-51.

could reduce the figure to 3.4 %. With these considerations in mind, it is difficult to draw any affirmative conclusion regarding the possibility of a Latin /b/ - /u̯/ merger in initial position in Dalmatia.

Data (for Dalmatia) from H. Mihăescu's study (*op. cit.*, Secs. 77-78) of the Latin of the Danubian provinces amount to a total of seventeen examples of the use of V for the expected Latin B spelling (five of which are in proper nouns), and an even larger number of examples of the use of B for the expected Latin V spelling — forty-four examples (thirteen of which are in proper nouns). From these data he concludes the existence of an intervocalic /b/ - /u̯/ merger in Dalmatia. I have assembled the data given by Mihăescu for this phenomenon in the following tables:

(a) *CLat.* B /b/

Interv. (B) → V	*Postcon.* (B) → V	*Verb End.* (B) → V	*Init.* (B) → V	*Tot. Dev.* (B) → V
16 (5)	0	1	0	17 (5) *

(b) *CLat.* V /u̯/

Interv. (B) → V	*Postcon.* (B) → V	*Verb End.* (B) → V	*Init.* (B) → V	*Tot. Dev.* (B) → V
16 (5)	5 (2)	8	15 (5)	44 (13) *

Mihăescu's general conclusion concerning the existence of a Latin intervocalic /b/ - /u̯/ merger in the Danubian provinces would seem to apply for the Latin of Dalmatia only, but we must remember that here it is not based on a quantitative-comparative analysis of the frequency of the B and V spellings and deviations therefrom. His conclusion is given greater substance by our analysis of the B and V spellings in the inscriptions from Dalmatia.

The development of a Latin intervocalic /b/ - /u̯/ merger appears to have been slower in Dalmatia than it was in North Africa, Gaul, and Italy (cf. *infra*), as we find many more deviations in spelling in these latter regions. The absence of a con-

---

* Indicates the number of deviations in proper nouns.

sistent pattern of deviations in dated inscriptions, as can be seen in our table, and percentage figures based on single deviations makes it rather difficult to establish the precise period for this change. However, if for no other reason, the large number of forms with interior *V* and deviations therefrom found in fifth and sixth-century inscriptions together would seem to justify treating these as one group in an attempt to determine a possible chronology of an intervocalic /b/ - /u̯/ merger in Dalmatia on the basis of inscriptional material. During this period there are a total of 41 occurrences of the expected interior *V* spelling and four deviations (or 8.8 %) with *B*. During this same period, there were twenty-five occurrences of the expected initial *V* and three deviations (or 10.7 %) with *B*. Could not the examples of the use of *B* for *V* initially and internally be interpreted as evidence that the stonemasons who cut the inscriptions under consideration really did not distinguish in their speech the two Latin consonants represented by these letters and that the development of a Latin intervocalic /b/ - /u̯/ merger was well underway or perhaps even completed in Dalmatia during the course of the fifth and sixth centuries?

The development of the intervocalic /b/ - /u̯/ merger in Dalmatian has geographical as well as chronological interest. Among the topics in Romance linguistics which have generated lasting and animated discussion is the question of a possible regional partitioning of spoken Latin, as reflected in the modern Romance languages. A special point in this controversy has been the validity of making an East-West division of Romance speech on the basis of certain linguistic features.[14]

---

[14] The term "West" Romance will, for the sake of simplicity, refer to the entire Romance dialect area of Western Europe except central and southern Italy, Sicily, Corsica, and Sardinia, although from the technical point of view there are reasons for not excluding Sardinia. The term "East" Romance will, for the sake of simplicity, refer to the Romance dialect area of Europe which comprises central and southern Italy, Sicily, Corsica, Sardinia, and Rumania, although from the technical point of view there are reasons for not including Sardinia. See M. A. Pei, "Intervocalic Occlusives in 'East' and 'West' Romance," *Romanic Review*, XXXIV (1943), 235-247. In this article, Pei calls into question the criteria used by some scholars for a general distinction between "East" and "West" Romance. See also, Walter von Wartburg, *Die Ausgliederung der romanischen Sprachräume* (Bern, 1950), especially pp. 60 ff.

In a *mise au point* entitled *The Phonological History of Vegliote*, [15] R. Hadlich attempts to reassess the entire problem of Vegliote's position among the Romance languages, according to the methods of diachronic structuralism. While it would be outside the scope of this study to discuss this scholar's line of reasoning, suffice it to say that Hadlich seems to advance some cogent and lucid arguments to support his conclusion [16] that "we must consider Vegliote rather a linguistic system in which according to the normal criteria, the East-West division of the Romance languages does not apply" (p. 83). He observes that some important features of the historical evolution of the consonantal system of Vegliote parallel those of "East" Romance, whereas the evolution of the vocalic system is similar to that of "West" Romance. Hadlich addresses himself to this dichotomy of the Dalmatian vocalic and consonantal systems in the following manner when he writes:

> Thus the Vegliote vowel system developed like those of the West Romance languages and the consonant system like those of the East Romance languages. This situation resulted from the chronology of the changes which characterize the West Romance languages. That is, the changes characteristic of the West Romance vowel system had already taken place (including Vegliote Latin) by the time that Veglia was isolated from the West by the Slavs. However, the Western consonant changes took place considerably after this isolation so that West Romance influence on changes in Veglia were impossible. (pp. 68-69)

Some might consider the early merger of Latin /b/ and /u̯/ as constituting a regional isogloss for some parts of central southern Italy, Corsica, Sardinia, Sicily, and Rome (*infra*, Secs. 13 and 14). In Dalmatia, the phenomenon in question appears not to have

---

[15] R. Hadlich, *The Phonological History of Vegliote*, University of North Carolina Studies in the Romance Languages and Literatures, No. 52 (Chapel Hill, North Carolina: University of North Carolina Press, 1965).

[16] See Thaddeus Fergusson, "A History of the Romance Vowel Systems Through Paradigmatic Reconstruction" (unpublished Ph.D. dissertation, Department of French and Romance Philology, Columbia University, 1970), pp. 222-246. In these pages, Fergusson calls into question Hadlich's method of tracing the evolution of the Vegliote vowel system.

developed as quickly and as early as it did in other areas (North Africa, Gaul, Italy). The eventual merger of intervocalic /b/ and /u̯/ in Dalmatia, observed on the basis of inscriptional material, would seem to indicate that there is no discernible "East"/"West" division with respect to this phenomenon.

5.3 Conclusions

(1) A Latin intervocalic /b/ - /u̯/ merger seems to have occurred in Dalmatia during the course of fifth/ sixth centuries.

(2) The existence of a Latin intervocalic /b/ - /u̯/ merger was a very widespread phenomenon (cf. *infra*.), comprising areas otherwise classified under "East" and "West" Romance dialect areas. There is no discernible "East"/"West" Romance distinction with respect to this phenomenon.

(3) In Dalmatia, the Latin /b/ and /u̯/ participated in an intervocalic merger, a phenomenon which affected all areas of the Western Roman Empire where Romance speech later developed. Here, the evolution of the Latin /b/ and /u̯/ (intervocalic) differs from the evolution of these two consonants in the inland Balkan Peninsula.

10. NORTH AFRICA

1. Intervocalic Position

1.1. CLat B /b/

Area	Century	(B) → B	(B) → V	%
Africa	III	4	0	
	IV	17	1	
	V	11	0	
	VI	14	0	
	VII	1	2	66.2
	n. d.	67	1	
	Totals	114	4	3.3

Sporadic occurrences of the use of the letter *V* for *B* occur in intervocalic position in the inscriptions from Africa. The only deviation in fourth-century material occurs in the form AVITA-

TIO (= HABITATIO) (*D.* 1830 a. 379/388). In seventh-century inscriptions we find the Latin intervocalic /b/ represented by the letter *V* two times out of a total of only three possible occurrences, a rather scanty sampling. The 66.2 % figure is rather misleading and may not represent the state of affairs, since the two deviations are found in the form CUVICULARIO, both on the same inscription (*D.* 359). As with all cases of single deviations, these may merely represent the errors of a single stonemason. The danger of attaching too much importance to an example of this type is clear.

Except for a single *V* spelling for intervocalic /b/ in the dative/ablative plural pronominal form NOVIS (= NOBIS) (*D.* 2339), Latin /b/ in this position always appears correctly spelled *B* throughout undated inscriptions from Africa.

1.2. CLat. V /u̯/

Century	(V) → V	(V) → B	%
III	4	0	0.0
IV	12	3	20.0
V	23	0	0.0
VI	17	8	32.0
VII	0	0	0.0
n. d.	63	26	29.3
Totals	119	37	23.7

In fourth-century inscriptions, deviations are found in the following forms:

    IUBANTE (*D.* 1830 a. 379/388)
    BIBIT (= VIVIT) (*D.* 3309A. a. 354)
    FABENTE (*D.* 3339 a. 352)

In sixth-century inscriptions *B* spellings for intervocalic /u̯/ are found in the following forms:

    BIBOQUE (*D.* 785 VI cent.)
    AIUBANTE (= ADIUVANTE) (*D.* 795 a. 578/582)
    IUBANTE (*D.* 747 VI cent.)
    PROBIDENTIA (*D.* 804b a. 539/540)
    FABENTE, CIBITAS, and PROBIDENTIA, all on the same inscription (*D.* 805 a. 539/540)
    TABESTINAE (*D.* 2043 VI cent.), a proper noun

THE B-V ALTERNATION IN LATIN INSCRIPTIONS 61

Following are some examples of deviations in undated incriptions:

> BIBAT (= VIVAT) (D. 869)
> IOBIANUS (= IOVIANUS) (D. 1188)
> PROBINCIE (= PROVINCIAE) (D. 1346)
> NOBE (= NOVEM) (D. 1349A)
> NOBEMBRES (= NOVEMBRIS) (D. 1393; D. 2096; and the abbreviated form NOB) (D. 1831, et passim)
> VITRUBIA (D. 1388A)
> DATIBA (D. 1407A)
> REBOCATUS (D. 2041)
> [PR]IBATA (D. 2048)
> VIBAS (D. 2218)
> IUBA (= IUVANTE) (D. 2437)
> OCTABU (D. 3052A)

The 32.0 % figure in sixth-century inscriptions is reduced to 27.2 %, since it includes three deviations on the same inscription. These may represent the orthography of a single stonemason. It would be well to note that 17 out of a total of thirty-six deviations occur in proper nouns, which generally lend themselves to more frequent misspellings than do common nouns used in daily communication. Even if we leave these items out of our count, there would still be a 13.7 % deviation over-all. This is still convincing as to an intervocalic /b/ - /u̯/ merger.

Despite the lack of deviation in fifth and seventh-century inscriptions, the 12 % progression in percentage figures in the sixth century over the fourth century, coupled with all reliable instances of *B* spellings to represent Latin intervocalic /u̯/ in undated inscriptions, indicate that of the four peripheral areas of the Roman World, it is Africa which shows the largest percentage of *B* spellings for the Latin /u̯/ in the intervocalic position. As for the significance of these spellings, there would seem to be little doubt that they reflect the merger of the Latin intervocalic /b/ and /u̯/. Africa, then, distinguishes itself as the least conservative peripheral Latin speaking area as compared with Britain, the Balkans, and (to a less extent) Dalmatia with regard to the treatment of the Latin /b/ and /u̯/.

2. Postconsonantal Position

2.1. CLat. B /b/ after /r/

Century	(-LB-) → -LB-	(-LB-) → -LV-
III	0	0
IV	1	0
V	0	0
VI	0	0
VII	0	0
n. d.	1	0
Totals	2	0

There are only two occurrences of words with the expected -*LB*- spelling and no deviations.

2.2. CLat. B /b/ after /r/

Century	(-RB-) → -RB-	(-RB-) → -RV-
III	0	0
IV	0	0
V	0	1
VI	2	0
VII	0	0
n. d.	0	0
Totals	2	1

In our corpus of inscriptions from Africa, there are only two cases of the expected -*RB*- spelling, and one deviation with -*RV*- in the form ACERVA (*D.* 2815B a. 475).

2.3. CLat. B /b/ after /s/.

Century	(-SB-) → -SB-	(-SB-) → -SV-
III	0	0
IV	1	0
V	2	0
VI	1	0
VII	0	0
n. d.	9	3
Totals	13	3

There are thirteen cases of the expected -*SB*- spelling in our inscriptional material from Africa. The three examples of the

THE *B-V* ALTERNATION IN LATIN INSCRIPTIONS 63

use of *-SV-* for *-SB-* are found on undated inscriptions, and are limited to the form PRESVITER for PRESBITER (*D.* 1184; *D.* 1590; *D.* 1601).

2.4. CLat. *V* /u̯/ after /l/

Century	(-LV-) → -LV-	(-LV-) → -LB-
III	0	0
IV	2	0
V	4	1
VI	1	0
VII	0	0
n. d.	16	4
Totals	23	5

There are twenty-three cases of the expected *-LV-* spelling in our corpus of inscriptions from Africa and five deviations (two in proper nouns) with *-LB-*. The only example of *-LB-* for *-LV-* in dated inscriptions occurs in the form PULBERI (*D.* 3477 a. 455/456). In undated inscriptions we found:

SILBANIANUS (*D.* 214)
SALBATORIS (*D.* 802)
SOLBIT (= SOLVIT) (*D.* 1896)
SALBU (= SALVO) (*D.* 2482)

2.5. CLat. *V* /u̯/ after /r/

Century	(-RV-) → -RV-	(-RV-) → -RB-
III	0	0
IV	2	0
V	0	1
VI	0	1
VII	0	0
n. d.	7	5
Totals	9	7

There are nine cases of the expected *-RV-* spelling in our corpus of inscriptions from Africa. In dated inscriptions, the examples of the use of *-RB-* for *-RV-* are:

RESERBOR (*D.* 3477 a. 455/456)
SERBUS (*D.* 1457 a. 538/539)

The five -RB- spellings for -RV- in dated inscriptions are:

SERBUS (D. 1185)
SERB. (= SERVUS) (D. 1456)
SERBU (D. 1619A; D. 1976B)
BERBA (= VERVA) (D. 2412)

2.6. CLat. V /u̯/ after /n/.

Century	(-NV-) → -NV-	(-NV-) → -NB-
III	0	0
IV	1	0
V	1	1
VI	2	0
VII	0	0
n. d.	7	6
Totals	11	7

In the inscriptions from Africa, there are eleven cases of words with the expected -NV- and seven deviations (six in undated inscriptions) with -NB-. (There is one example of -NB-, correctly spelled.) In dated inscriptions, -NB- for -NV- occurs in the form INBENITUR (D. 3477 a. 455/456). In undated inscriptions deviations occur in the following forms:

INBIDIA and INBIZIOSA (D. 2388A)
INBIDE (= imperative of INVIDERE) (D. 2388C)
INBIDET (D. 2476). In a garbled inscription full of incomprehensible words we read INBICTA and INBIZAINARIOS (D. 2388B)

2.7. CLat. V /u̯/ after /d/

In our corpus of inscriptions from Africa, there are five cases of words with the expected -DV- (/du̯/), all in undated inscriptions; hence the absence of any tabular representation. The examples of the use of -DB- for -DV- (a total of three) all occur in undated inscriptions and are limited to the proper noun QUODVULTDEUS, which appears variously spelled.

QUODBULUS (D. 945)
CODBUL (D. 1411)
CODBULDEU (D. 2720)

2.8. SUMMARY: *The B-V Alternation in Postconsonantal Position*

What appears to be decidedly characteristic of the spelling of the expected B and V in postconsonantal position in the inscriptions from Africa is an inconsistency in the use of these two letters after /d/, /l/, /n/, /r/, and /s/. In order to show the number of instances of confusion in the use of these two letters in this particular position, we give a summary table of total correct occurences and deviations. (In the heading, the capital C stands for *Consonant*.)

Century	(-CB-) → -CV-		%	(-CV-) → -CB-		%
III	0	0		0	0	
IV	2	0		5	0	0.0
V	2	1		5	3	37.5
VI	3	0		3	1	(25.0)
VII	0	0		0	0	
n. d.	11	3	21.4	35	19	35.1
Totals	18	4	18.3	48	23	31.4

A lack of consistency in the use of the V spelling for the expected Latin B spelling is to be noted. In dated material there is only one deviation out of a total of seven possible occurrences. This does not necessarily mean that in this particular area a postconsonantal /b/ - /u̯/ merger may not have been well along its way as evidenced by the 18.3 % figure over-all.

Since the high percentage (18.3 %) of V spelling for B in this position reflects a postconsonantal /b/ - /u̯/ merger in Africa, we might expect to find the opposite phenomenon, viz. Latin postconsonantal /u̯/ appearing as B. Indeed, we do find a number of examples of this spelling, about six times the number of V for B. If we leave a total of five B spellings for V in proper nouns out of out total count, we get a 26.1 % figure. The high percentage of V spellings for the expected B, and the even higher percentage of B spellings for the expected V in postconsonantal position (both well over the five percent control figure) are evidence that this alternation has its source in some kind of phonological change. The presence of an intervocalic /b/ - /u̯/ merger suggests that in this region there was also a postconsonantal /b/ - /u̯/ merger.

3. Verb Endings

3.1. CLat B /b/ in Future Tense Endings

Latin /b/ occurs in the first, second, and third persons singular future active indicative only. There are only a total of ten occurrences of this consonant in these endings and three deviations (one each in the above mentioned persons) with *V*. The ratio of correct occurrences and deviations is as follows:

    A. 1st person singular
    B. 2nd person singular
    C. 3rd person singular

Century	A (-BO)	→-VO	B (-BIS)	→VIS	C (-BIT-)	→-VIT	Tot. Cor.	Tot. Dev.	%
III	0	0	0	0	0	0	0	0	
IV	0	0	1	1	0	0	1	1	
V	1	0	0	0	0	0	1	0	
VI	0	0	0	0	0	0	0	0	
VII	0	0	0	0	0	0	0	0	
n. d.	4	1	1	0	3	1	8	2	20.0
Totals	5	1	2	1	3	1	10	3	23.0

Examples of the *V* spellings for *B* found in connection with these personal endings of the future tense are, from the fourth century:

    VIDEVIS (= VIDEBIS) (D. 1830)

from undated inscriptions:

    TIMEVO (= TIMEBO) (D. 2410)
    VALEVIT (= VALEBIT) (D. 791)

3.2. CLat V /u̯/ in perfect tense endings of REQUIE-VIT → REQUIE-BIT, and of other verbs as well

In this section, data concerning the Latin *V* are restricted to the third person singular perfect tense ending of REQUIESCERE and of other verbs. The sampling of Latin *V* in this tense ending is frequent, due to the frequent occurrence of the stereotyped death formula HIC REQUIEVIT IN PACE, which is characteristic of the inscriptions from this area. As can be seen from the following table, deviations outnumber the correct forms. The ratio of correct occurrences and deviations is as follows:

Century	(-VIT) → -VIT	(-VIT) → BIT	%
III	0	0	
IV	3	0	
V	4	1	(20.0)
VI	3	3	50.0
VII	0	0	0.0
n. d.	25	34	57.6
Totals	35	38	52.1

Latin /u̯/ is spelled *B* a total of thirty times in the stereotyped form REQUIEVIT. This form appears variously spelled REQUIE-BIT (*D.* 3139 a. 453), QUIEBIT (*D.* 3104A a. 510), QYIEBIT (*D.* 549), CU[I]EBIT (*D.* 3095), QUIEPI (*D.* 1943), REQUIEDIT (*D.* 3141A). The latter two forms are isolated cases, and would seem to be due to a stonecutter's error. The remaining eight examples (all in undated inscriptions) of *B* for *V* in this tense ending of other verbs are:

> CONPLEBIT (*D.* 527)
> MILITABIT (*D.* 549)
> FABRICABIT (*D.* 778)
> DURAB[I]T (*D.* 1111)
> DORMIBIT (*D.* 1389)
> EXIB[IT] (*D.* 2773; *D.* 2884)
> PAUSABIT (*D.* 3243)

3.3. CLat. *V* /u̯/ in other perfect tense endings and in other verb endings

Data concerning Latin *V* /u̯/ in these endings are given in the following table. It will be seen that occurrences of the /u̯/ are infrequent and, in the perfect tense, deviations are limited to the first and third persons plural. In other verb endings (where no cases of the /u̯/ occur), we found a single deviation in the third person plural, future perfect active indicative/perfect active subjunctive (both endings are represented in Classical Latin by the form -*VERINT*). On the following page we give the ratio of correct occurrences and deviations:

68 THE EVOLUTION OF THE LATIN /b/ - /u̯/ MERGER

3.3a. The Latin (V) /u̯/ in other verbal endings

A. first person singular perfect active indicative
B. first person plural perfect active indicative
C. third person plural perfect active indicative
D. third person plural future perfect active indicative/ perfect active subjunctive

Century	A (-VI)→-BI	%	B (-VIMUS)→-BIMUS	%	C (-VERUNT)→-BERUNT	%	D (-VERINT)→-BERINT	Tot. Cor.	Tot. Dev.	%
III	0		0		0		0	0	0	
IV	0		0		1		0	1	0	
V	0		0		4		0	4	0	
VI	0		1		0		0	0	2	
VII	0		0		0		0	0	0	
n. d.	2		1		4		1	6	3	33.3
Total	2	0	2		9	18.1	1	11	5	31.3

3.2b. CLat V /u̯/ in Other Perfect Tense Endings and in Other Verb Endings

(a) *First Person Singular Perfect Active Indicative*

There are two occurrences of this verb ending with the V and no deviations.

(b) *First Person Plural Perfect Active Indicative*

There are no occurrences of the expected V in this verb ending, but there are two deviations with B. These are limited to the verb form AEDIFICAVIMUS, which appears spelled as EDIFIKBIMUS (*D.* 793 a. 582), and EDIF[I]CABIMUS (*D.* 800), no date.

(c) *Third Person Plural Perfect Active Indicative*

There are a total of nine occurrences of the expected V spelling in this ending, and two deviations with B. One of these occurs in a sixth-century inscription and reads EDIFIKBERUNT (*D.* 793 a. 582), and the other in an undated inscription and reads COMPLEBERUNT (= COMPLEVERUNT) (*D.* 1917).

(d) *Third Person Plural Future Perfect Active Indicative/ Perfect Active Subjunctive*

There are no occurrences of this verb ending with the V, but there is one deviation in an undated inscription in the form PUTEBERINT (= PUTAVERINT) (*D.* 1003).

3.4. SUMMARY: The Latin V /u̯/ in All Perfect Tense Endings and in Other Verb Endings Together

Data concerning Latin V /u̯/ in these verb endings are shown in the following table. The purpose of this table is twofold:

(a) to show deviations from the expected V, and
(b) to summarize the data concerning the use of B to represent /u̯/ in these verb endings as contributory evidence of a merger of /b/ and /u̯/ in the intervocalic position in Africa.

Our criteria in this connection (as it will be in other areas where this procedure will be observed, viz. Italy, including Rome) will be the total number of correct occurrences of the *V* in these verb endings and deviations therefrom. The ratio of correct occurrences and deviations is as follows:

Century	(V) → B		%
III	0	0	
IV	4	0	0.0
V	8	1	(11.1)
VI	3	5	62.5
VII	0	0	
n. d.	31	37	54.4
Totals	46	43	48,3

The 11.1 % figure in fifth-century inscriptions may be misleading, since it is based on a single deviation which may represent the error of a single stonemason. The high percentage figure (62.2 %) in sixth-century inscriptions is based on a total of only five deviations with *B* as against three cases of the expected *V* spellings in these verb endings (a rather small sampling). But, these data, together with the number of examples of the use of *B* for *V* (which outnumber the correct forms) in undated inscriptions, and the 48.3 % over-all figure leave little doubt that an intervocalic /b/ - /u̯/ merger was an accomplished fact in Africa.

4. *Initial Position*

4.1. CLat. *B* /b/

Century	(B) → B	(B) → V	%
III	1	0	
IV	17	0	
V	8	0	
VI	4	0	
VII	3	0	
n. d.	98	4	3.9
Totals	131	4	2.9

Four examples of the use of *V* for initial *B* occur in the inscriptions from Africa. All deviations (one in a proper noun) are found in undated inscriptions, and are limited to forms of the adjective BONUS, -A, -UM. They are:

VONE (= BONAE) (D. 1294)
VONIFATIA (= BONIFATIA) (D. 1403A)
VONO (= BONUM) (D. 2036)
VONA (= BONA, in the phrase PAX DEI VONA CARITAS) (D. 2497A)

4.2. CLat. V /u̯/

Century	(V) → V	(V) → B	%
III	3	0	0.0
IV	66	1	1.5
V	73	2	2.7
VI	23	4	14.8
VII	0	0	0.0
n. d.	367	69	15.8
Totals	532	76	12.5

Deviations in dated inscriptions occur in the following forms, from the fourth century:

BIBIT (= VIVIT) (D. 3309A a. 354)

The examples of deviations from the fifth century are found in proper nouns only. They are:

BALERIUS (= VALERIUS) (D. 1110 a. 482)
BILLATICA (= VILLATICA) (D. 3139 a. 453)

From the sixth century we found:

BIBOQUE (= VIVOQUE) (D. 785 VI cent.)
BIGOR (= VIGOR) (D. 795 a. 578/582)
BIRI (= VIRI) (D. 539/540)
BINCENTI (= VINCENTI) (D. 2043 a. 503/548)

By far the most frequent examples showing a *B* spelling for initial *V* in undated inscriptions are found in the verb form VIXIT, which appears variously spelled BIXIT (D. 233), BISIT (D. 1184), BIXXIT (D. 1247), BICXIT (D. 1346), and BICSIT (D. 2835). In fact, one-half (34 in number) of all deviations found in undated inscriptions from Africa are limited to this verb form, which one would expect to be least likely to be misspelled, because it usually occurs in stereotyped formulae. The correct form VIXIT also occurs frequently. Thus, we find IN PACE BIXIT (*D.* 389B), but VIXIT IN PACE (*D.* 389A), from the same region (Tunetana-Uppenna, North Africa). Examples of deviations in other than this verb form are:

BOTUM (= VOTUM) (*D.* 527)
BICTOR (= VICTOR) (*D.* 1406)
BERBA (= VERVA) (*D.* 2412)
BOLUMTATIS (= VOLUNTATIS, in the phrase PAX HOMINIBUS BONAE BOLUMTATIS) (*D.* 2463)
BULNERA (= VULNERA) (*D.* 2388C)
BICIT (= VICIT, 3rd person, singular, present perfect active indicative of VINCERE)
BENERANDE (= VENERANDAE) (*D.* 2089)

5. Summary and Conclusions

We may now attempt to summarize our data concerning the use of *B* and *V* in the inscriptions from Africa, to see if they shed any light on the possibility of an intervocalic /b/ - /u̯/ merger in this area. The criteria in this connection will be the percentage of *V* spellings for interior /b/ and the percentage of *B* spellings to represent interior /u̯/. To the extent that our data permit, we will also attempt to establish a possible chronology of intervocalic /b/ - /u̯/ merger in Africa. In order to show the reader the trend of this merger, and, in anticipation of a comparison between our data from Africa with those from other areas of the Western Roman Empire, we give the following summary tables:

Century	(B) → V		%	(V) → B		%
III	4	0	0.0	4	0	0.0
IV	20	2	9.1	21	3	12.5
V	14	1	(6.1)	36	4	10.0
VI	17	0	0.0	23	14	37.8
VII	1	2	66.3	0	0	0.0
n. d.	86	6	6.5	129	82	38.8
Totals	142	11	7.1	213	103	32.6

5.1. SUMMARY: The Latin /b/ and /u̯/ in the Interior Position

Data concerning the Latin interior *B* spelling in dated inscriptions would seem to show that the Latin /b/ retained its occlusive articulation and showed little sign of weakening. The 9.1 % figure in fourth-century inscriptions may be misleading, since it is based on only two deviations as against twenty cases of *B*. The 6.1 % figure in fifth-century inscriptions is based on a single deviation. This may represent the error of a single stonemason. The 66.3 % figure in seventh-century inscriptions may not represent the state of affairs, since it is based on only a single occurrence of the expected *B* and two deviations with *V*. However, the number of instances in which the interior *B* is represented by *V* in dated and undated inscriptions together (142 cases of *B* and eleven, or 7.1 % with *V* is sufficient evidence to indicate a Latin /b/ - /u̯/ merger in this position in Africa.

On the other hand, we note a low reliability in representing the Latin interior /u̯/. *B* spellings for original /u̯/ begin to appear in Africa in the fourth century, and continue through the sixth. Contrary to our data concerning the interior *B*, parallel data for the *V* in seventh-century inscriptions shows 0.0 %. These extremes are obviously due to the fact that there are only a total of three possible cases of *B* in our inscriptions, and none with *V*. The over-all 32.6 % figure clearly indicates a Latin interior /b/ - /u̯/ merger in this area. If we leave a total of twenty-two deviations in proper nouns out of our count, we get a 27.5 % figure. This is also conclusive evidence of a merger in the interior position of the two Latin consonants represented by the letters *B* and *V*.

5.2. SUMMARY: *The Latin /b/ and /u̯/ in the Initial Position*

It would be difficult to determine the possibility of a Latin /b/ - /u̯/ merger in initial position based on deviations (2.9 %) from the expected spelling of the initial /b/ alone. However, the 12.9 % figure showing the use of *B* for initial /u̯/ shows such a merger. As in the interior position, *B* spelling for initial /u̯/ begin in the fourth century and increase in number through the sixth. We have no way to check the accuracy of our conclusion, since Latin did not survive in Africa in the form of a Romance language, and there is no testimony available from ancient Latin grammarians which speaks of the phonemic status of Latin initial /b/ and /u̯/ in this area.

We may now address ourselves to the question of the possible chronology of intervocalic /b/ - /u̯/ merger in Africa. We note that interior *V* spellings for *B* and vice versa make their appearance in Africa around the middle of the fourth century. Other dated examples occur around the middle of the fifth century. If we take the total correct occurrences of the interior *B* /b/ — 34 and three deviations with *V* during this period — we arrive at an 8.1 % figure. Our figures show an even lower reliability in representing the interior /u̯/ during this period. The use of *B* for *V* — 4 examples as against 57 cases of the expected *V* spelling, or 10.9 % — indicates that a Latin /b/ - /u̯/ merger in the interior position was well underway during the course of the fourth/fifth centuries. That the phenomenon in question was an accomplished fact by the sixth century is clear from the 37.8 %.

5.3. *Conclusions*

Although S. W. Omeltchenko (*op. cit.*, p. 457, ff) finds that the vocalism of the Latin spoken in Africa is conservative in nature,[17] very few deviations from the norms of classical Latin orthography having been noted, this state of affairs does not obtain for the *B* and *V* spelling for the Latin /b/ and /u̯/. According to the evidence of our inscriptional material, we may sum up our findings as follows:

(1) Deviations from the expected *B* and *V* spellings amounting to more than five percent in interior and initial positions indicate a Latin /b/ - /u̯/ merger in these positions.

(2) The treatment of the Latin /b/ and /u̯/ in Africa is less conservative than the treatment of these two consonants in Britain and Balkans (and to a lesser extent, Dalmatia), thereby establishing

---

[17] Attention has already been given to matters concerning the possibility of an African dialectal variant of spoken Latin, which now seems to be a matter of historical interest. See P. Gaeng (p. 292, and note 8) and S. W. Omeltchenko (pp. 56-59).

a regional differentiation with respect to the phenomenon in question.

(3) The merger of the Latin intervocalic /b/ and /u̯/ in Africa parallels the evolution of these two consonants in the Vulgar Latin of other areas of the Western Roman World, viz. Spain, Gaul and Italy (cf. *infra*). A complete merger here parallels that of Rome and Southern Italy.

11. SPAIN

1.1. CLat. *B* /b/

Area	Century	(B) → B	(B) → V	%
Baetica	IV/VI	4	0	
	VII	13	1	
	n. d.	5	0	
	Totals	22	1	4.3
Lusitania	IV/VI	8	1	
	VII	2	0	
	n. d.	1	0	
	Totals	11	1	8.3
Tarraconensis	IV/VI	9	0	
	VII	7	0	
	n. d.	5	0	
	Totals	21	0	0.0

Following are the examples of deviations.

(a) *Baetica*. There were twenty-two occurrences of the expected intervocalic *B* spelling. The only deviation found in the inscriptions from Baetica occurs in the form OVIT (= OBIIT) (*V*. 114).

(b) *Lusitania*. There were eleven occurrences of the expected *B* spelling and one deviation with *V*. This occurs in the form DEVITUM (*V*. 291 a. 593).

(c) *Tarraconensis*. There were twenty-one occurrences of the expected intervocalic *B* spelling and no deviations.

The absence of a consistent pattern of deviations in dated inscriptions, as can be seen from the tables, and a 3.6 % over-all figure based on 54 occurrences of the expected B and only two deviations with V (one each of which occurs in Baetica and Lusitania only), would seem to indicate that the Latin intervocalic /b/ was stable in Spain. We must investigate the Latin interior /u̯/, in order to determine, on an over-all basis, the possibility of an intervocalic /b/ - /u̯/ merger.

1.2. CLat. V /u̯/

Area	Century	(B) → B	(B) → V	%
Baetica	IV/VI	6	2	25.0
	VII	8	1	(11.0)
	n. d.	3	2	40.0
	Totals	17	5	22.7
Lusitania	IV/VI	7	2	22.2
	VII	4	0	
	n. d.	3	0	
	Totals	14	2	12.5
Tarraconensis	IV/VI	14	2	12.5
	VII	7	1	(14.2)
	n. d.	4	1	(20.0)
	Totals	25	4	13.7

(a) *Baetica.* In dated inscriptions the use of the letter B for the expected intervocalic V occurs in the following forms:

    OCTABO (V. 134 a. 562)
    CIBITATE (V. 364 a. 573)
    IUBENIS (V. 179 a. 663)

In undated inscriptions deviations occur in the following forms:

    [BR]EBE (= BREVE) (V. 508)
    IUBENTUDIS (= IUVENTUTIS) (V. 381)

The number of occurrences of Latin intervocalic /u̯/ is small, so that the high percentage of deviations (22.7 %), based on seventeen correct occurrences of the expected V spelling and five deviations with B, seems to indicate a Latin intervocalic /b/ - /u̯/

merger in this area. In view of the scanty sampling at our disposal, this percentage may or may not reflect the state of affairs.

(b) *Lusitania.* The following two forms found on the same inscription from the fifth century show a *B* spelling for the Latin intervocalic /u̯/:

> NOBABIT (= NOVAVIT), NOBANTE (Vives suggests either NOVANTE or NOVATA) (V. 363 a. 483)

Since these two forms may represent the orthography of a single stonemason, the 12.5 % over-all figure may not represent the state of affairs, and it would be difficult to say just how complete a possible merger of intervocalic /b/ with /u̯/ may have been (or even if such a merger existed) in this area on the basis of these two deviations alone.

(c) *Tarraconensis.* In dated inscriptions the following examples of *B* spellings for intervocalic /u̯/ occur:

> OBES (= OVIS "sheep") (V. 283 VI cent.)
> PROBIDENS (V. 356 a. 529/534)
> NOBEM (V. 314 a. 661)

In undated inscriptions there is one example of the use of *B* for *V* in the form CAPTIBIS (V. 278).

The 13.7 % figure based on four instances in which the intervocalic /u̯/ is represented by *B* as compared with twenty-five correct classical spellings points in the direction of a development which eventually resulted in the merger of /b/ and /u̯/ in the intervocalic position.

2. *Postconsonantal Position*

2.1. CLat. *B* after /l/

Area	Century	(-LB-) → -LB-	(-LB-) → -LV-
Baetica	IV/VI	0	0
	VII	0	0
	n. d.	0	0
	Totals	0	0

78 THE EVOLUTION OF THE LATIN /b/ - /ṷ/ MERGER

Area	Century	(-LB-) → LB-	(-LB-) → -LV-
Lusitania	IV/VI	0	0
	VII	0	0
	n. d.	0	0
	Totals	0	0
Tarraconensis	IV/VI	0	0
	VII	0	0
	n. d.	0	0
	Totals	0	0

In the Christian inscriptions from Spain, words with -LB- do not occur.

2.2. CLat. *B* after /r/

Area	Century	(-RB-) → -RB-	(-RB-) → -RV-
Baetica	IV/VI	0	0
	VII	2	0
	n. d.	1	0
	Totals	3	0
Lusitania	IV/VI	1	0
	VII	0	0
	n. d.	0	0
	Totals	1	0
Tarraconensis	IV/VI	2	0
	VII	2	0
	n. d.	0	1
	Totals	4	1

As can be seen from the tables, there were only a total of eight occurrences of words with -RB- in Spain and one deviation. This was found on an undated inscription from the Tarraconensis area in the form ACERVOS for an expected ACERBOS (V. 292).[18]

---

[18] We did not include two instances of the often cited ARVITER < ARBITER (*V.* 281 and *V.* 282) because, according to Vives, the inscriptions on which these forms are found are of uncertain origin ("De procedencia incierta (Asturias?)"). A. Carnoy, *Le latin d'Espagne d'après les inscriptions,* 2ed. (Louvain: J. B. Istas, 1906), p. 146, finds that in the inscriptions from Asturias most of the examples of *V* for *B* after *R* or *L* are found; whereas in the other provinces *RV* and *LV* for *RB* and *LB* are almost

2.3. CLat. V. after /l/

Area	Century	(-LV-) → -LV-	(-LV-) → -LB-
Baetica	IV/VI	2	0
	VII	2	0
	n. d.	0	0
	Totals	4	0
Lusitania	IV/VI	0	1
	VII	0	0
	n. d.	0	0
	Totals	0	1
Tarraconensis	IV/VI	0	1
	VII	0	0
	n. d.	0	0
	Totals	0	1

(a) *Baetica.* There were only four occurrences of words with -LV- and no deviations.

(b) *Lusitania.* There were no occurrences of words with the expected -LV-, but there was one deviation with -LB- on a fifth-century inscription in the form SOLBERAT (*V.* 363 a. 483).

(c) *Tarraconensis.* As in Lusitania, there were no occurrences of words with the expected -LV-, but there was one deviation with -LB- in a sixth-century inscription in the form FULBIDA (*V.* 356 a. 529/534).

---

unknown, the opposite spelling being more frequent. The inscriptional data for this phenomenon, all of unknown dates, cited by Carnoy amount to the following: two examples of ARVITER for ARBITER; VARVIUS < VARBIUS, BARBIUS;, ALVITIUS < ALBITIUS ("d'une époque plus ancienne"); ALVANUS < ALBANUS ("graphie suspecte"). The French scholar asks if these data can be taken as evidence of a weakening of Latin /b/ to /b/ after /l/ or /r/ in Spain at the same time as the intervocalic (b) - (ų) merger (*infra*, pp. 84-86). Three considerations stand in the way of an easy acceptance of these data as evidence of a weakening of postconsonantal /b/ at this time: (1) They are all of unknown dates; thus, we have no way of knowing if they reflect a weakening of postconsonantal /b/ at about the same time as the intervocalic /b/ - /ų/ merger in Spain; (2) one example (ALVANUS) is, according to Carnoy, of questionable spelling and would, therefore, not be totally reliable; and (3) there is an absence of quantitative data showing the frequency of occurrence of the expected *B* and *V* spellings after *L* and *R* and deviations therefrom.

2.4. CLat. V after /r/

Area	Century	(-RV-) → -RV-	(-RV-) → -RB-
Baetica	IV/VI	0	0
	VII	3	0
	n. d.	1	0
	Totals	4	0
Lusitania	IV/VI	0	0
	VII	0	0
	n. d.	0	0
	Totals	0	0
Tarraconensis	IV/VI	0	0
	VII	0	0
	n. d.	0	0
	Totals	0	0

As with words with *-LV-*, occurrences of words with *-RV-* are found in the inscriptions from Baetica only. There are no examples of *-RB-* spellings for *-RV-* in the inscriptions from Spain.

3. CLat V /u̯/ in REQUIE-VIT → REQUIE-BIT, and in the perfect tense of other verbs

Area	Century	(-VIT) → -VIT	(-VIT) → -BIT	%
Baetica	IV/VI	1	0	
	VII	5	0	
	n. d.	1	0	
	Totals	7	0	0.0
Lusitania	IV/VI	40	4	9.0
	VII	12	0	0.0
	n. d.	1	0	0.0
	Totals	53	4	7.0
Tarraconensis	IV/VI	2	4	66.6
	VII	5	1	(13.2)
	n. d.	3	0	0.0
	Totals	10	5	33.3

Examples of *B* for *V* in perfect tense endings are as follows:

(a) *Baetica.* There were only seven occurrences of the *-VIT* ending and no deviations.

(b) *Lusitania.* The number of occurrences of the *-VIT* ending in this area is largely due to the fact that the consecrated expression is HIC REQUIEVIT IN PACE. (In Baetica and Tarraconensis, HIC REQUIESCIT IN PACE is the characteristic formula.) The four deviations in fourth/sixth-century inscriptions are found in the forms NOBABIT and FUNDABIT, both on the same fourth-century inscription (*V.* 363 a. 483), and REQUIEBIT/REQIEBIT, on one and the same sixth-century inscription (*V.* 52a/b a. 566).

The 9.0 % figure in fourth/sixth-century inscriptions from this area should be regarded with caution. We find that the expected *V* (/u̯/) in perfect tense endings is represented by *B* four times as against forty correct classical spellings. Would it be logical, therefore, to conclude that this figure reflects an intervocalic /b/ - /u̯/ merger by this time in Lusitania? Any kind of general statement in this regard is highly questionable and hypothetical since:

(1) this figure and the 7.0 % over-all figure is not supported by deviation in seventh-century inscriptions or in undated inscriptions.

(2) two *B* spellings for Latin /u̯/ in this ending occur in the stereotyped verb from REQUIEVIT in the very same inscription. These two deviations need not surprise us when we consider the numerous similar examples of the use of *B* for /u̯/ in this verb form in other areas as well. As with all cases of single deviations, they may represent the spelling of a single stonemason only.

(3) two more *B* spellings in other werbs also occur on the same inscription and may also represent the errors of a single stonemason.

(4) all four deviations were found on inscriptions from the same region (Mérida) and may represent a localism. We found one occurrence of the ending *-VERUNT* correctly spelled in our fourth/sixth-century inscriptional material.

(c) *Tarraconensis.* Examples of *-BIT* for *-VIT* in Tarraconensis are as follows:

> ORNABIT, MINISTRABIT (*V.* 279 VI cent.)
> MELLIFICABIT (*V.* 282 a. 558)
> REPLEBIT (*V.* 284 a. 558)
> LOCABIT (*V.* 285 a. 630)

The 66.6 % figure in fourth/sixth-century inscriptions from this area is rather misleading since (1) the /u̯/ is represented by *B* four times out of a total of only six possible occurrences; and (2) the *B* for *V* in the forms ORNABIT and MINISTRABIT are found on the same inscription and, hence, may represent the spelling of a single individual only. But, while the data concerning the use of *B* to represent /u̯/ in perfect tense endings in this area may not be conclusive as to a possible Latin intervocalic /b/ - /u̯/ merger, they can be indicative of such a possibility.

4. Initial Position

4.1. CLat. *B* /b/

Area	Century	(B) → B	(B) → V	%
Baetica	IV/VI	16	0	
	VII	13	0	
	n. d.	4	0	
	Totals	33	0	0.0
Lusitania	IV/VI	6	0	
	VII	0	0	
	n. d.	1	0	
	Totals	7	0	0.0
Tarraconensis	IV/VI	8	0	
	VII	5	0	
	n. d.	1	1	
	Totals	14	1	(6.6)

(a) *Baetica.* There are thirty-three occurrences of the expected initial *B* and no deviations.

(b) *Lusitania.* There are only seven occurrences of the expected initial *B* and no deviations.

(c) *Tarraconensis.* The only example of an initial *V* spelling for *B* is found in the Tarraconensis area on an undated inscription in the expression

VISQUE (= BISQUE) QUATERNIS MENSIBUS (*V*. 279)

Data concerning the spelling of the Latin /b/ in initial position show that there are a total of 54 occurrences of the expected B spelling and only one deviation with V in the form VISQUE. On the basis of the spelling of the Latin initial /b/, we believe that this consonant was quite stable in this position in Spain. But let us also investigate data concerning the initial Latin /u̯/.

4.2. CLat. V /u̯/

Area	Century	(V) → V	(V) → B	%
Baetica	IV/VI	51	0	
	VII	43	0	
	n. d.	14	0	
	Totals	108	0	0.0
Lusitania	IV/VI	71	0	
	VII	11	0	
	n. d.	9	0	
	Totals	91	0	0.0
Tarraconensis	IV/VI	51	1	
	VII	4	0	
	n. d.	24	1	
	Totals	79	2	2.4

Example of the use of B for initial V occur in the Tarraconensis area only, more particularly in the Tarragona (Northeastern Spain) region. They are:

BIXIT (V. 214) from the fifth century
BALERIA (= VALERIA) (V. 269), no date

Among all Christian inscriptions from Spain under investigation, there were only two examples of the use of B for V to represent initial /u̯/, and one of these occurs in a proper noun which is, of course, of doubtful significance because of a possible lack of orthographic tradition. Furthermore, these two deviations are from the same restricted area (a Tarragona cemetery) and may represent a localism.

On the basis of 278 correct occurrences of the expected initial V spelling and only one reliable deviation, we would be justified in stating that the Latin initial u̯ was quite stable in Spain during the periods covered by the inscriptions.

THE EVOLUTION OF THE LATIN /b/ - /u̯/ MERGER

Evidence of stability of initial /b/ and of initial /u̯/ means an absence of merger of the two in initial position, i.e., the conservation of the phonemic distinction.

5. Summary and Conclusions

We may now attempt to summarize our data concerning the Latin /b/ and /u̯/ in Spain.[19] The criteria in this connection will be the total percentage of V spellings for the interior /b/ and the total percentage of B spellings for the interior /u̯/. We will also attempt to establish a possible chronology of the intervocalic /b/ - /u̯/ merger in Spain on the basis of inscriptional material. We summarize our findings in tabular form:

5a. Comparative Tables Concerning the Treatment of Latin /b/ and /u̯/ in the Interior Position

Area	Century	(B) → -V		%	(V) → -B		%
Tarraconensis	IV/VI	11	0		16	7	30.4
	VII	9	0		12	2	14.2
	n. d.	5	1		7	1	(12.2)
	Total	25	1		35	10	22.2
Baetica	IV/VI	4	0		9	2	18.2
	VII	15	1		18	1	(5.2)
	n. d.	6	0		5	2	28.5
	Total	25	1	(3.1)	32	5	13.5
Lusitania	IV/VI	10	1		47	7	12.8
	VII	2	0		16	0	0.0
	n. d.	1	0		4	0	0.0
	Total	13	1	(6.6)	67	7	9.5

---

[19] In view of our anticipation of a possible extension of the intervocalic /b/ - /u̯/ merger westward from Tarraconensis, we are modifying our geographical breakdown (adapted from Gaeng) and will present data on the intervocalic /b/ - /u̯/ merger in Spain in the following order: Tarraconensis, Baetica, and Lusitania, i.e., from the easternmost area to the westernmost area.

5.1 SUMMARY: *The Latin /b/ and /u̯/ in the Interior Position*

As can be seen in the tables, deviations from the expected Latin *B* spelling are few. Percentage figures (3.1 % in Tarraconensis and Baetica, and 6.6 % in Lusitania) based only on single deviations in these areas would make any kind of general statement regarding the stability of the Latin interior /b/ in Spain highly questionable and hypothetical. We must turn to our data concerning the *B* spellings for *V* in order to determine, on an over-all basis, the possibility of a Latin intervocalic /b/ - /u̯/ merger in Spain.

(a) *Tarraconensis.* The percentage figures given in the table show a low reliability in representing the Latin interior /u̯/. Here the Latin /u̯/ is represented by *B* in 22.2 % of the cases (10 deviations as compared to 35 expected classical *V* spellings). On the basis of our findings, the Tarraconensis area, more especially the Northeastern part (since the bulk of the inscriptions come from here), i.e., what is today the area of Catalonia, shows the highest percentage of *B* spellings for the /u̯/ (cf. *infra*) and would seem to be least conservative in its treatment of the interior /u̯/.[20] It is also to be noted that as we move westward, the percentage figures decrease, possibly indicating that the phenomenon may have begun in Tarraconensis and spread in that direction. It is also possible that this occurred spontaneously in the different regions (see Italy, Sec. 5.2).

(b) *Baetica.* The 13.5 % figure is sufficient evidence (32 correct occurrences of the expected *V* and five deviations with *B*) to indicate a Latin intervocalic /b/ - /u̯/ merger in this area. Are we to interpret the single deviation in seventh-century inscriptions as a result of a sudden conservative influence in this area, or as a result of a particularly carefully written group of inscriptions?

---

[20] Innovations in the Eastern Tarraconensis area (precisely the area where the Catalan language developed) with regard to matters concerning vocalic developments were found and have already been pointed out by Gaeng (pp. 68, 96, and 98). Our findings with respect to the intervocalic /b/ - /u̯/ merger in the Tarraconensis area parallel those of Gaeng and would seem to lend support to this scholar's suggestion (p. 98, note 60) that our inscriptional material may point to an early dialectal separation of this area from the rest of the Spanish Peninsula.

There is no reason to think that a further search would not turn up several more cases where *B* and *V* show some alternation.

(c) *Lusitania*. The 9.5 % figure over-all (67 cases of the expected *V* and seven deviations with *B*) would, at least, seem to indicate that a Latin intervocalic /b/ - /u̯/ merger had begun in this area during the period covered by the inscriptions. How are we to interpret the decrease in the percentage of deviations in seventh-century inscriptions to zero? The fact that there were only sixteen occurrences of the interior /u̯/ in this century, i.e., one-third of the occurrences with respect to the previous centuries, may be offered as an explanation.

Dated inscriptions from Spain seem to point to about the middle of the sixth century as the approximate time of this merger, although it may have taken place at an earlier time, possibly about the first quarter of this century, at least in Tarraconensis, on the basis of some specifically dated inscriptions.

R. L. Politzer undertook an investigation of a number of Latin documents from Aragon, Castile, and Leon, written approximately between 980 and 1090, published by Menéndez-Pidal in his *Orígenes del Español*.[21] In this study, Politzer gives quantitative and comparative data on the use of *B* to represent the intervocalic /u̯/. In the documents from Aragon he records the highest percentage of deviations — 100 % (six deviations with *B* as against no occurrences of the expected *V*), 48 % (13 examples of *B* to 14 occurrences of the expected *V* spelling) in the documents from Castile, and 48 % (17 examples of *B* to 19 cases of the expected *V*) in the documents from Leon. He does not give data concerning the use of *V* to represent intervocalic /b/. Politzer's conclusion (p. 64) that "intervocalically the opposition [between /b/ and /u̯/] is neutralized," seems to be underway by at least the middle of the sixth century, and perhaps earlier.

Data concerning the use of *B* to represent intervocalic /u̯/ in the inscriptions from Spain already show clear-cut evidence of the geographical extension of the intervocalic /b/ - /u̯/ merger, similar to that observed by Politzer in the later documents, namely its apparent origin in the eastern part of the Peninsula, and its west-

---

[21] "On the Development of the Latin Stops in Aragonese," *Word*, X (1954), 60-65.

ward spread. We may also consider the possibility that the phenomenon in question may have developed spontaneously at different times in the various regions of Spain.

5.2 SUMMARY: *The Latin /b/ and /u̯/ in Initial Position*

The contrast in the data concerning the use of *B* and *V* to represent Latin initial /b/ and /u̯/ is well illustrated by a comparison of our inscriptional material and Politzer's tenth/eleventh-century documents from Spain (*supra,* Sec. 5.1). It will be recalled that there were no examples of an initial *B-V* confusion in the inscriptions from Baetica and Lusitania. In Tarraconensis two examples of the use of *B* for initial *V* were found; and one of these is in a proper noun, so that the original 2.4 % figure is reduced to 1.3 %. It is clear that on the basis of the inscriptions, the Latin initial /b/ and /u̯/ remained distinct in Spain during the periods covered by our inscriptions. In regard to this, J. Carnoy's observation, namely that "On n'a donc aucune raison de faire remonter la confusion entre *b* et *v* du Castillan récent jusqu'au Latin vulgaire,"[22] finds strong support in the inscriptions.

On the other hand, Politzer's documents show a 100 % use of the letter *B* for initial /u̯/ in Aragon (24 deviations with *B* as against no cases of the correct classical spelling); a 6 % figure in Castile (three deviations with *B* as compared with forty-three cases of the expected *V* spelling), and a 2 % figure in Leon (one deviation with *B* as against 76 occurrences of the expected *V* spelling). Politzer concludes: "in Aragonese *v* as a separate phoneme has ceased to exist. In Castilian and Leonese, on the other hand, ... the two phonemes still alternate initially" (p. 64). He does not give data concerning the use of *V* for initial *B*.

It must be pointed out that Politzer's use of the heading *(V) → B* is quite different from its use in the present work. In his study it is to be interpreted as evidence of a merger of the Castilian /b/ and /v/ in word-initial position into a single voiced bilabial phoneme in contrast with the majority of Romance languages and dialects which keep labial occlusive and labial fricative phonemes distinct in initial position. In his study, Politzer at-

---

[22] A. Carnoy, *Le latin d'Espagne d'après les inscriptions,* pp. 141-144.

tempts to show the similarity between this phenomenon in Castilian and Basque. He does not, however, raise the question of a possible influence of a Basque substratum, as there seems to have been,[23] to account for the origin of this phenomenon in Castilian. Since the inscriptions do not come from the area inhabited by the Basques, data given under the heading *(V) → B* are to be interpreted as mistakes, and not as evidence of a possible beginning of the Castilian initial /b/ - /v/ merger.

It is not the intention of the present writer to put in doubt Carnoy's observation (*op. cit.*, p. 135) accepted by later generations of Romanists that "En dehors de la Gaule, il n'y a pas de province où *b* pour *v* soit aussi peu répandu qu'en Espagne." However, only a cursory reading of inscriptional material would lead to such a statement. His observation is, we believe, too general and might be re-examined.

A review of the data concerning the use of *B* and *V* in initial position in the inscriptions under investigation in the present study reveals that reliable examples showing the use of initial *B* for *V* are as few in Britain as they are in Spain and are totally absent in the provinces of the inner Balkans (*supra*, Sec. 7, 4.1; Sec. 8, 4.1, 4.2. We need only reproduce the findings of the present quantitative and comparative analysis of inscriptional material and compare the number of forms showing the use of *B* for initial *V* in Gaul and Spain with these former areas to show that the inscriptions do not support Carnoy's claim. We give a summary table of total correct occurrences and deviations:

---

[23] The most lucid and thorough presentation of this subject according to the methods of diachronic phonemics is F. H. Jungemann's: *La Teoría del sustrato y los dialectos Hispano-Romances y Gascones*, trans. D. Emilio Alarcos Llorach (Madrid: Editorial Gredos, 1955). In this work (Chapter XV), Jungemann attributes the complete merger of the /b/ and /v/ in Hispano-Romance to the influence of a Basque substratum. He writes: "Estos fenómenos podrían haberse originado por el bilingüismo eusquera-romance" (p. 360). This merger seems to have begun in Castilian and spread to other areas with the spread of Castilian as the official language.

Area	(V) → B		%	(B) → V		%	Total Deviation
Gaul	478	6	1.2	215	0	0.0	6
Spain	278	2*	0.7	54	1	(1.8)	3
Britain (Pagan/Christ.)	454	2*	0.4	80	0	0.0	2*
Balkans (Pagan/Christ.)	183	0	0.0	41	1	(2.4)	1

Carnoy's generalization seems to need modification to the effect that (1) on the basis of inscriptions, the number of forms showing the use of *B* for initial *V* is the same in Britain as it is in Spain; (2) this phenomenon would be "peu répandu" in the provinces of the inner Balkans where examples of *B* for initial *V* are totally absent; and (3) there are fewer examples of the use of *B* for initial *V* in Spain than in Gaul.

5.3 Conclusions

It is now clear that neither the time element nor the geographical extension of the intervocalic /b/ - /u̯/ merger in Spain are problematical. We may summarize our findings as follows:

(1) The Latin intervocalic /b/ - /u̯/ merger seems to have been well underway (if not completed) in Spain by, at least, the middle of the sixth century, thus foreshadowing a later, clearer delineation as reported in Politzer's study of tenth/eleventh-century Latin documents from Spain.

(2) The highest, consistent percentage difference of deviations occurs in Tarraconensis, more especially the Northeastern region, i.e., what is today the Romance dialect area of Catalonia.

(3) The origin and existence of an intervocalic /b/ - /u̯/ merger in other areas of Spain may be a result of a westward spread of the phenomenon from Tarraconensis. This may, however, have simply begun spontaneously at different times in the three regions.

---

* On the same inscription. The figure in parenthesis (under *Total Deviation*) indicates the actual number considered, i.e., two deviations found on the same inscription are counted as one.

(4) The Latin initial /b/ and /u̯/ are quite stable in Spain, on the basis of data from the inscriptions. There is no evidence that the later merger of the Spanish /b/ and /v/ in all positions is to be attributed to any peculiarity of the Latin of Spain.

12. GAUL

1. *Intervocalic Position*

1.1 CLat. B /b/

Area	Century	(B) → B	(B) → V	%
Lugdunensis	IV/V	19	4	17.3
	VI/VII	28	5	15.1
	n. d.	32	11	25.5
	Totals	79	20	20.2
Narbonensis	IV/V	9	0	0.0
	VI/VII	49	5	9.3
	n. d.	17	0	0.0
	Totals	74	5	6.3

(a) *Lugdunensis.* A high percentage of deviations with respect to the Latin intervocalic /b/ were found in the inscriptions from Lugdunensis. Following are deviations from dated inscriptions, from the fifth century:

> OVIIT (= OBIIT) (*D.* 306 a. 448; *D.* 1551 a. 447)
> LIVERTUS (= LIBERTOS) (*D.* 1749 a. 487)
> PROVATA (= PROBATA) (*D.* 3488 a. 498)

from the seventh century:

> NUVELIS (= NOBILIS), LAUDAVELIS (= LAUDABE-LIS), CONSCRIVERE (= CONSCRIBERE), and NUVI-LIOR (= NOBILIOR, a comparative adjective form), all appearing on the same verse inscription to honor a church personality (*D.* 1075 a. 630). The latter form appears in an inscription of similar content as NOVILIOR (*D.* 1076 a. 630)

In undated inscriptions we found the following forms in which Latin intervocalic /b/ is represented by the letter *V*:

> OVIIT (*D.* 53)
> OVIET (*D.* 2902; *D.* 2902A; *D.* 3529)
> LIVER (= LIBER) (*D.* 483)
> LIVELIS (= LIBELIS) (*D.* 3567)
> LIVIRI (= LIBERI) (*D.* 4827)
> LEVERTO (*D.* 1616b)
> FLIVELIS (= FLIBELIS) (*D.* 3567). The dative/ablative plural form OMNIBUS appears written twice as OMNEVOS (*D.* 4824; *D.* 4827).

(a) *Narbonensis*. In this area the over-all percentage of deviations is only about one-third of that found in the Lugdunensis, in approximately the same amount of material. The following forms found in sixth/seventh-century inscriptions from the Narbonensis area show a *V* spelling for Latin /b/ in intervocalic position:

> NOVELETATE (= NOBILITATE) (*D.* 270 a. 562/563)
> OVIET, OVIIT (*D.* 2889A a. 524; *D.* 3550 a. 528), respectively
> SIVI (= SIBI) (*D.* 3580 ca. VI/VII cent.)

The high percentage of *V* spellings for intervocalic /b/ leaves little doubt that the merger of /b/ and /u̯/ in the intervocalic position was an accomplished fact in Gaul during the periods covered by the inscriptions.

1.2 CLat. *V* /u̯/

Area	Century	(V) → V	(V) → B	%
Lugdunensis	IV/V	11	1	
	VI/VII	6	0	
	n. d.	29	1	
	Totals	46	2	4.2
Narbonensis	IV/V	8	0	0.0
	VI/VII	13	2	13.3
	n. d.	9	1	(10.0)
	Totals	30	3	9.1

(a) *Lugdunensis.* In fourth/fifth-century inscriptions the only B spelling for V in intervocalic position is found in the form

VIBATIS (= VIVATIS) (*D.* 2207)

On an undated inscription we found B for intervocalic V in the form

IOB. (= IOVIANUS) (*D.* 1970M)

(b) *Narbonensis.* In the inscriptions from Narbonensis, we found only three examples of B for intervocalic V. In sixth/seventh-century inscriptions deviations occur in the following forms:

OCTABO (= OCTAVO) (*D.* 2021 a. 521)
IUBENTE (= IUVENTE) (*D.* 3438 a. 506)

In undated inscriptions a single example of B for intervocalic V is found in the form

IUBENIS (= IUVENIS) (*D.* 3421)

The sporadic occurrences of B spelling for V in intervocalic position in Gaul (4.2 % on the basis of only two deviations in Lugdunensis and 9.1 % on the basis of only three deviations in Narbonensis) would make it difficult to draw any general conclusions regarding the stability of the Latin /b/ in this position, if it were not for the numerous misspellings of the intervocalic /b/ just noted above.

The contrast in the data concerning the use of the B and V in Gaul is well illustrated by the fact that in the Narbonensis the percentage of V spellings for intervocalic B is about one-third of that in the Lugdunensis, but the percentage of B spellings for intervocalic V is about twice that in the Lugdunensis. (The possible inferences to be drawn from this will be discussed in the summary, *supra,* Sec. 5.3).

2. Postconsonantal Position

2.1 CLat. B after /l/

Area	Century	(-LB-) → -LB-	(-LB-) → -LV-
Lugdunensis	IV/V	0	0
	VI/VII	0	0
	n. d.	0	0
	Totals	0	0
Narbonensis	IV/V	0	0
	VI/VII	0	0
	n. d.	1	0
	Totals	1	0

(a) *Lugdunensis*. In this area forms with *-LB-* do not occur.

(b) *Narbonensis*. As can be seen from the table, there is only one occurrence of the expected *-LB-* spelling in this area and no deviations.

2.2 CLat. B after /r/

Area	Century	(-RB-) → -RB-	(-RB-) → -RV-
Lugdunensis	IV/V	0	0
	VI/VII	0	1
	n. d.	2	0
	Totals	2	1
Narbonensis	IV/V	1	0
	VI/VII	2	0
	n. d.	4	0
	Totals	7	0

(a) *Lugdunensis*. The only *-RV-* spelling for *-RB-* in this area is found in the form VERVIS (= VERBIS) (*D.* 1075 a. 630). In undated inscriptions there is one example of the use of *-SV-* for *-SB-* in the form PRESVITER (*D.* 2177).

(b) *Narbonensis*. There are no deviations in either dated or undated inscriptions from this area.

2.3 CLat. V after /l/

Area	Century	(-LV-) → -LV-	(-LV-) → -LB-
Lugdunensis	IV/V	1	0
	VI/VII	1	0
	n. d.	1	0
	Totals	3	0
Narbonensis	IV/V	0	0
	VI/VII	0	0
	n. d.	1	0
	Totals	1	0

(a) *Lugdunensis*. There are only three occurrences of the expected *-LV-* spelling and no deviations.

(b) *Narbonensis*. There is only one occurrence of the expected *-LV-* spelling and no deviations.

2.4 CLat. V after /r/

Area	Century	(-RV-) → -RV-	(-RV-) → -RB-
Lugdunensis	IV/V	1	0
	VI/VII	1	0
	n. d.	1	0
	Totals	3	0
Narbonensis	IV/V	0	0
	VI/VII	1	0
	n. d.	3	0
	Totals	4	0

(a) *Lugdunensis*. There are three words with the expected *-RV-*, and no deviations with *-RB-*.

(b) *Narbonensis*. There are four words with the expected *-RV-*, and no deviations with *-RB-*.

THE B-V ALTERNATION IN LATIN INSCRIPTIONS 95

3. *CLat.* V /u̯/ *in perfect tense endings, e.g.,* REQUIE-VIT → REQUIE-BIT *(and other verbs as well)*

Area	Century	(-VIT)→-VIT	(-VIT)→-BIT	%
Lugdunensis	IV/V	3	1	(25.0)
	VI/VII	3	0	
	n. d.	7	4	36.3
	Totals	13	5	27.7
Narbonensis	IV/V	0	0	0.0
	VI/VII	7	1	(12.8)
	n. d.	8	2	20.0
	Totals	15	3	16.6

(a) *Lugdunensis.* The only B spelling for V in perfect tense endings in dated inscriptions is found in the form REQUIEBIT (D. 3559 a. 492). In undated inscriptions, the four examples of deviations occur in the following verb forms:

ORDINABIT (D. 282)
LABORABIT (D. 1586)
REQUIEBIT (D. 3559)
PORTABIT (D. 4010)

(a) *Narbonensis.* The only example of the use of -BIT for -VIT in dated inscriptions occurs in the form FONDABET (D. 1808 a. 530). In undated inscriptions we found REQUIEBIT (D. 3289) and DICABIT (D. 3579).

4. *Initial Position*

4.1 CLat. B /b/

Area	Century	(B) → B	(B) → V
Lugdunensis	IV/V	14	0
	VI/VII	33	0
	n. d.	51	0
	Totals	98	0
Narbonensis	IV/V	7	0
	VI/VII	64	0
	n. d.	43	0
	Totals	117	0

(a) *Lugdunensis*. Latin initial /b/ is universally spelled B in this area. On the basis of inscriptions it would seem that Latin /b/ was pronounced in Lugdunensis as /b/ in initial position.

(b) *Narbonensis*. The inscriptions from this area show no examples of the use of the letter V for B in initial position. The high reliability in the spelling of the initial /b/ indicates that this consonant was quite stable in this position.

4.2 CLat. V /u̯/

Area	Century	(V) → V	(V) → B	%	Other
Lugdunensis	IV/V	40	0		
	VI/VII	57	0		
	n. d.	169	2	1.1	*1* (V) → F
	Totals	266	2	0.8	
Narbonensis	IV/V	28	0	0.0	
	VI/VII	75	2	2.6	
	n. d.	109	2	1.8	
	Totals	212	4	1.9	

(a) *Lugdunensis*. The Latin initial /u̯/ occurs frequently in this area, partially due to the frequent occurrences (a total of 157) of the stereotyped form VIXIT followed by a numeral to denote the number of years the deceased person has lived. There occur two instances (both in the verb form VIXIT) in which the Latin initial /u̯/ is represented by B. These occur in undated inscriptions only:

BIXIT (*D.* 1317)
BICSIT (*D.* 3112A)

The other deviation is found in the form FIXIT (= VIXIT) (*D.* 2803C), which, seeing this is an isolated case, would seem to be due to a stonecutter's error.

According to the evidence of the inscriptions, in which Latin initial /u̯/ appears almost universally represented by V, we would be justified in concluding that this consonant is quite stable in initial position in this area.

(b) *Narbonensis*. The sampling for Latin initial /u̯/ is also quite frequent, due to the frequent occurrence (a total of 119) of the stereotyped form VIXIT followed by the age of the deceased. In the main, the /u̯/ in this position is represented by *V*, although an occasional *B* spelling is found. The four deviations are limited to the verb form VIXIT. They are, from the sixth century:

> BIXIT (*D*. 2891 a. 527)
> BI[XIT] (*D*. 3472 a. 568)

from undated inscriptions:

> BISSIT (*D*. 2257)
> BIXIT (3541)

As can readily be seen from the tables, the occurrence of a *B* spelling for initial /u̯/ is very sporadic and the overwhelming majority of occurrences of the correct spelling indicates that the Latin /u̯/ in initial position was quite stable in Gaul during the periods covered by our inscriptions.

From the point of view of chronology, it would be well to note that deviations from the expected *B* and *V* spelling in the Narbonensis do not occur earlier than the first quarter of the sixth century, contrary to what we observe in the Lugdunensis, a fact which may have some significance.

5. *Summary and Conclusions*

We will summarize our data concerning the treatment of the Latin /b/ and /u̯/ in Gaul. To the extent that we are able, we will also attempt to establish a possible chronology of the intervocalic /b/ - /u̯/ merger in Gaul on the basis of inscriptions.

5a. *Comparative Tables Concerning the Treatment of the Latin* /b/ *and* /u̯/ *in the Interior Position in Gaul*

Area	Century	(B) → V		%	(V) → B		%
Lugdunensis	IV/V	19	4	17.3	16	2	11.1
	VI/VII	28	6	17.6	11	0	
	n. d.	34	11	24.4	38	6	13.5
	Totals	81	21	20.6	65	8	10.9
Narbonensis	IV/V	10	0	0 0	8	0	0.0
	VI/VII	51	5	8.9	21	3	12.5
	n. d.	22	0	0.0	21	4	16.0
	Totals	83	5	5.7	50	7	11.1

5.1 SUMMARY: *The Latin /b/ and /ṷ/ in the Interior Position*

(a) *Lugdunensis*. In fourth/fifth-century inscriptions from Lugdunensis the Latin interior /b/ is represented by V four times as against nineteen correct spellings with B, or 17.3 %. A similar state of affairs obtains in sixth/seventh-century inscriptions. The interior /b/ is spelled with V six times as against twenty-eight correct occurrences, or 17.6 % The conclusion that a Latin intervocalic /b/ - /ṷ/ merger was an accomplished fact by the time of the appearance of our Christian Latin inscriptions from this area is justified.

In the eighth-century texts from Northern Gaul (i.e., *grosso modo* the area of Lugdunensis), M. A. Pei [24] finds that the majority of V spellings for Latin /b/ "appear in a number of cases in the intervocalic position" (p. 94) and attributes the V spelling in this position to a weakening of the Latin intervocalic /b/. A glance showing the treatment of the Latin intervocalic /b/ in inscriptions will show us that Pei's findings are foreshadowed in the inscriptions from Lugdunensis.

On the other hand, the results of the investigation of the B spelling for V would seem to be in agreement with those of Pei who found "only three examples of the reverse spelling of B for V" (p. 95). In dated inscriptions, there are not enough B spellings for V in the intervocalic position alone to enable us to establish a consistent pattern or trend. To the extent that we are able to draw any conclusions regarding a possible intervocalic /b/ - /ṷ/ merger on the basis of inscriptions, there would seem to be some justification to treat the total occurrences of the interior V (/ṷ/) and deviations therefrom together. In this position there occur a total of 65 correct V spellings for the interior /ṷ/ and 7 deviations (or 9.7 %) with B. As for the significance of the B spellings for the /ṷ/, there would seem to be little doubt that they reflect the merger of /b/ and /ṷ/ in the intervocalic position.

Pei sums up his conclusions regarding the alternation between intervocalic B and V when he writes:

---

[24] M. A. Pei, *The Language of the Eighth-Century Texts in Northern France*.

The state of affairs in our own and other texts would seem to indicate that a state of hesitation prevailed in the Eighth Century, probably indicating the merging of the two sounds in pronunciation (p. 95).

(b) *Narbonensis*. The results of the investigation of the interior *V* to represent Latin /b/ in Narbonensis show a total of 83 occurrences of the expected *B* spelling and five deviations (or 5.7 %) with *V*. On the other hand, the figures for the interior /u̯/ (*V*) show an even lower reliability in the spelling of this consonant. There occur 50 expected *V* spellings and six deviations (or 10.7 %) with *B*. Both figures are conclusive as to a merger of intervocalic /b/ and /u̯/ in this area.

It will be observed that data concerning the use of *B* and *V* in our Christian Latin inscriptions from Gaul show that the use of *V* for intervocalic *B* is more frequent in the inscriptions from Lugdunensis than it is in those from Narbonensis. In Narbonensis, as in all other provinces, *B* spellings for *V* are more frequent. The question is, does this skewing in favor of *V* spellings for *B* consequent on an intervocalic merger in Lugdunensis have implications for our analysis of the Latin intervocalic /b/ and /u̯/? Can one take this skewing as an indication of possible regional differences? Consistency in the use of *V* for *B* in this position might suggest the existence of such a possibility. If so, Lugdunensis would be most innovating in this respect.[25]

However, a possible structural explanation may also be considered. We know that Latin intervocalic /p, t, k/ became voiced as /b, d, g/ everywhere in the Western Romance dialect area, but not in Eastern Romance (Central and Southern Italy and the Romanized Balkan regions).[26] We wonder whether the change Latin /-p-/ > /-b-/ took place earlier in Northern France (and Northern Italy, cf. *infra*), thereby setting off a weakening of the original Latin intervocalic /b/ in these two regions where the inscriptions show less *B* for original /u̯/, than in other regions. If

---

[25] Innovations in Lugdunensis with regard to matters concerning vocalic development have already been pointed out by P. Gaeng (pp. 53, 275).

[26] See M. A. Pei, "Intervocalic Occlusives in 'East' and 'West' Romance"; and M. K. Pope, *From Latin to Modern French* (Manchester University Press, 1934), Sec. 336.

so, we could consider a relationship as possible, but only in the time of the earlier inscriptions. Data from our inscriptions from Lugdunensis give some support to this hypothesis, but not much. In fourth/fifth-century inscriptions we found eleven cases of the expected intervocalic *-P-* spelling and no deviations with *-B-*; in sixth/seventh-century inscriptions we found ten cases of the expected intervocalic *-P-* spelling and one deviation with *-B-*. This occurs in the name of the month of April, which appears spelled as ABRILIO (*D*. 2456 VII cent.); in undated inscriptions we found sixteen cases of the expected intervocalic *-P-* spelling and one deviation with *-B-*. This occurs in the form LABIDEM (*D*. 202). The 5.1 % figure, based on a total of thirty-seven cases of the expected intervocalic *-P-* spelling and two deviations with *-B-* is just over the five percent control figure, and may perhaps be indicative of even a slight voicing of Latin intervocalic /-p-/. Nowhere in the inscriptions from Lugdunensis do we find forms with a *-V-* where Latin originally had a *-P-*.

In the Latin inscriptions from Gaul, Jules Pirson [27] points out an inconsistency on the part of stonemasons from Gaul in representing the Latin intervocalic /-p-/. The data given by Pirson were taken from his own and from several other studies of inscriptional material. He gives eight reliable examples of the use of *-B-* for an expected intervocalic *-P-*. These data amount to the following: two examples from the seventh century, and six of unknown dates. Pirson concludes that "une modification dans la prononciation de la sourde intervocalique" is responsible for the misspellings. There are, however, two considerations which stand in the way of an easy acceptance of this conclusion: (1) It is based on data gathered from several different sources and these independently may not give sufficient evidence of a possible voicing of intervocalic /-p-/ > /-b-/. (2) There is an absence or quantitative data showing the frequency of occurrence of the expected intervocalic *-P-* spelling and deviations therefrom. But these data cannot be discarded.

There is some evidence of voicing in eighth-century documents from Northern France. Pei (*Texts*, p. 92) finds only "a limited number of cases of the change of *p* to *b* in the intervocalic posi-

---

[27] Jules Pirson, *La Langue des inscriptions latines de la Gaule*, p. 60.

THE B-V ALTERNATION IN LATIN INSCRIPTIONS

tion," and concludes (p. 94) that the voicing of the intervocalic /-p-/ > /-b-/ "was still in progress in the early part of the Eighth Century." We cannot say how much earlier than this the voicing of intervocalic /-p-/ > /-b-/ had actually begun, though the inscriptions seem to give a clue. Pei gives no words with a -v- where the original Latin form had a -p-.[28]

In a study of a collection of Merovingian documents, dated 626-717,[29] R. L. Politzer gives quantitative data concerning a possible general voicing of Latin intervocalic /p, t, k/. He does not give data concerning a possible voicing of the individual voiceless consonants. He finds no examples of voicing in documents from the first half of the seventh century and very few in those of the second half (1.2 %), but a sharp increase in their frequency in those from 700 to 717 (4.9 %).

In sum, some evidence of the use of -B- for intervocalic -P- in the inscriptions may indicate that there may have been a slight amount of voicing of /-p-/ > /-b-/. There may be a possible connection between this phenomenon and the much less use of B for original /u̯/ in the inscriptions from Lugdunensis. The data are not strong enough to permit us to do more than to suggest this as a possibility.

5.2 SUMMARY: *The Latin /b/ and /u̯/ in the Initial Position*

(a) *Lugdunensis*. There were 98 cases of initial B and no V for initial B. There were 266 cases of the expected initial V and only two deviations (or a negligible 0.8 %) with B in the verb form VIXIT. The high reliability in the spelling of the initial /b/ and /u̯/ leaves little doubt that these two consonants remained distinct in this position. The results of our own investigation of the Latin initial /b/ and /u̯/ are in agreement with the conclusions reached by J. Pirson, who (*op. cit.*, p. 61), notes an absence of confusion between initial B and V and takes this as evidence that "la majeure partie de la Gaule a continué a distinguer soigneusement ces deux consonnes." Pei makes no mention of an alterna-

---

[28] In the Oaths of Strasbourg (a. 842), we do find such an example: *savir* < SAPERE.

[29] "On the Chronology of the Simplification of Geminates in Northern France," *Modern Language Notes*, LXVI (1951), 521-527.

tion between *B* and *V* in initial position. By his silence on the subject, he leads us to infer that initial /b/ and /u̯/ remained distinct.

(b) *Narbonensis*. Data concerning the treatment of the initial /b/ and /u̯/ in Narbonensis parallel those of the Lugdunensis. There were a total of 117 occurrences of the expected initial *B* spelling and no deviations. There were 212 occurrences of the expected initial *V* spelling and only four deviations (or 1.9 %) with *B* all in the stereotyped form VIXIT, followed by the age of the deceased. In Narbonensis, as in Lugdunensis, the high reliability in representing the Latin initial /b/ and /u̯/ leads us to conclude that these two consonants remained distinct in this position in this area.

In Christian inscriptions from Gaul (specifically the Narbonensis area), Pirson *(ibid.)* cites only one example of the use of initial *V* for *B* in the form VENE (= BENE), and nine examples of the use of *B* for initial *V*. He records no examples of the use of *B* for initial *V* in Lugdunensis. Regarding the alternation in the use of these two letters in this position, Pirson writes:

> La rareté de ce phénomène à la syllabe initiale n'a pas lieu à nous surprendre; car seuls quelques dialectes du midi de la Gaule, ont étendu à la syllabe initiale la fusion du /B/ et du /V/. On remarquera également que tous les examples mentionnés ci-dessous proviennent du midi de la Gaule.

We are left wondering, of course, whether Pirson is already cautiously raising the question of a possible early dialectal separation of a part of the Narbonensis area from the rest of Gaul, i.e., whether the alternation in the use of initial *B* and *V* which he observed is to be taken as evidence of an incipient merger of the Romance /b/ and /v/ in initial position, which is known to have occurred in Spanish and Gascon and seems to have spread eastward from this latter region to some non-Gascon regions in Southwestern France during the Middle Ages.[30] The French scholar has

---

[30] See Gerhard Rohlfs, *Le Gascon: études de philologie pyrénéenne*. *Zeitschrift für Romanische Philologie*, 85 (1935), 81-82.

to leave the question open since his study is not based on comparative and chronological data.

Haudricourt and Juilland sum up their conclusions concerning the loss of the Romance initial /b/ - /v/ distinction in Bas-Languedoc, the area immediately to the east of Gascony: "Vers le XV⁰ siècle, nous voyons ce type de corrélation dépasser la Garonne et gagner le Bas-Languedoc. A cette époque, la confusion entre *b* et *v* à l'initiale se généralise dans cette région." [31] According to these scholars, then, the merger spread from Gascony.

F. H. Jungemann (*op. cit.*, pp. 348, 361) agrees with Haudricourt and Juilland regarding the existence of such a merger in Bas-Languedoc. He claims that the loss of the initial /b/ - /v/ distinction in this area is explainable only as due to a spreading from Gascony: "Su existencia en Bas-Languedoc sólo se explica como difusión desde Gascuña." While there is no question that a complete merger of the Romance initial /b/ and /v/ is characteristic of some dialects in Southwestern France, there is no evidence in the inscriptions of its beginning in Vulgar Latin.

5.3 Conclusions

The situation in Gaul may be summed up as follows:

(1) Orthographic deviations found in dated inscriptions indicate that a Latin intervocalic /b/ - /u̯/ merger was well underway, if not completed, in Lugdunensis by the middle of the fifth century. On the other hand, in Narbonensis, data from the inscriptions show no deviations from the expected spelling of the Latin /b/ and /u̯/ earlier than the middle of the sixth century. The implication of this evidence is important; it suggests that a Latin intervocalic /b/ - /u̯/ merger in Lugdunensis antedates the same phenomenon in Narbonensis by at least a century.

(2) The consistent pattern of deviations in date inscriptions from Lugdunensis beginning around the middle of the fifth century (17.3 %) and continuing into the following centuries (15.1 %), to-

---

[31] Haudricourt and Juilland, *Essai pour une histoire structurale du phonétisme français* (Paris: Klincksieck, 1949), p. 68. See also George Jochnowitz, *Dialect Boundaries and the Question of Franco-Provençal* (The Hague: Mouton, 1973), pp. 122-128.

gether with the 25.5 % figure in undated inscriptions and a 20.0 % figure over-all, is, we believe, sufficient evidence to indicate that a Latin intervocalic /b/ - /y̨/ merger was an accomplished fact in this area approximately three centuries prior to the appearance of Pei's eighth-century documents from Northern France.

(3) We found a predominance of V spellings for interior B in Lugdunensis (which may reflect the actual sound change); whereas in Narbonensis, as in all other regions, B spellings for V are more frequent. There may be a possible connection between an early voicing of Latin intervocalic /-p-/ > /-b-/ and the less frequent use of B for original /y̨/ in Lugdunensis.

13. Italy

1. *Intervocalic Position*

1.1 CLat. B /b/

Area	Century	(B) → B	(B) → V	%
Northern	IV/V	39	6	13.3
	VI/VII	10	0	0.0
	n. d.	36	2	5.3
	Totals	85	8	8.6
Central	III/IV	19	3	13.6
	V	12	1	(7.5)
	VI/VII	7	1	(12.5)
	n. d.	39	3	4.9
	Totals	77	8	8.3
Southern	III/IV	12	0	
	V	6	0	
	VI/VII	14	2	1.9
	n. d.	51	1	
	Totals	83	3	3.5

(a) *Northern*. V spellings for B are found in the following forms, from the fifth century:

> LAUDAVILIS (= LAUDABILIS) (D. 254)
> OVITU (= OBITUM) (D. 432; D. 812; D. 4852)
> INCONPARAVILI (= INCOMPARABILIS) and OVITU,
>   both on the same inscription (D. 894)

in undated inscriptions *V* for intervocalic *B* occurs in

>OVITUM (*D.* 826)
>HAVITE (*D.* 3349)

The over-all 8.6 % figure (based on eight deviations) for this area is enough evidence to show an identification of Latin intervocalic /b/ and /u̯/. The decrease in the percentage of deviation in sixth/seventh-century inscriptions may be due to the fact that there are only a total of ten cases of the /b/, i.e., one-fourth of the occurrences with respect to the previous centuries.

(b) *Central.* Examples of *V* spellings for *B* from third/fourth-century inscriptions are the following:

>PROVIANO (*D.* 1027)
>PROVINO (*D.* 3036 a. 345; *D.* 3036A a. 395)

from the fifth century:

>[PRO]VINO (*D.* 1667N a. 489)

from the seventh century:

>AVEA[T...] (= HABEAT) (*D.* 3848 a. 632/633)

from undated inscriptions:

>FAVENTE (*D.* 36)
>SAVINA (*D.* 2711B)
>FUNGEVAT (= FUNGEBAT, a third person singular imperfect indicative form) (*D.* 3874)

The 8.3 % figure (based on eight deviations) from the Central Italian area would seem to indicate a Latin intervocalic /b/ - /u̯/ merger. This figure, however, may be misleading, since five out of eight deviations occur in proper nouns, which generally lend themselves to more frequent misspellings than common words used in daily communication. If we leave these items out of our count, we get a 3.8 % figure based on only three reliable deviations. The data showing the use of *V* for intervocalic /b/ in the inscriptions from Central Italy are not sufficient to permit us to make any affirmative statement regarding the possibility of an intervocalic /b/ - /u̯/ merger in this area. In Sec. 1.2b we will investigate the *B* spellings for intervocalic /u̯/.

(c) *Southern*. All three deviations occur in proper nouns. In sixth/seventh-century inscriptions we found:

EUSEVIUS (*D.* 487 a. 549)
PROVI (= PROBIANUS) (*D.* 3082Ba a. 504)

In an undated inscription we found:

EUSEVIA (*D.* 3223a)

The over-all low percentage figure (3.5 %, based on only three deviations) does not permit us to draw any affirmative conclusion regarding a possible merger of intervocalic /b/ and /u̯/ in Southern Italy. Furthermore, the three *V* spellings for Latin /b/ are limited to proper nouns. These may be of doubtful significance because of a possible lack of orthographic tradition. In Sec. 1.2c we will investigate the *B* spellings for the expected *V* in this area to see if they give us any indication of an intervocalic /b/ - /u̯/ merger.

1.2 CLat. *V* /u̯/

Area	Century	(V) → V	(V) → B	%
Northern	IV/V	30	1	(3.2)
	VI/VII	20	3	13.0
	n. d.	32	14	30.4
	Totals	82	18	18.0
Central	III/IV	5	5	50.0
	V	7	1	(12.5)
	VI/VII	7	2	22.2
	n. d.	37	8	11.7
	Totals	56	16	22.2
Southern	III/IV	3	3	50.0
	V	8	2	20.0
	VI/VII	16	10	38.7
	n. d.	20	30	60.0
	Totals	47	45	48.9

(a) *Northern*. Examples of *B* for intervocalic *V* in dated inscriptions are the following:

> NOBE (= NOVEM) (*D.* 439 a. 434)
> IOBANTE (= IUVANTE) (*D.* 1854 VI/VII cent.)
> EABADAS (= EAVADAS) (*D.* 3879b VI/VII cent. ?)
> FABIOLUS (= FAVIOLUS) (*D.* 1256a a. 560)

Some of the fourteen examples from undated inscriptions are:

> VIBI (= VIVI) (*D.* 1337)
> BIBA (= VIVA) (*D.* 2287A)
> VIBERE (= VIVERE) (*D.* 4341)
> CIBIS (= CIVIS) (*D.* 4451A)
> IOBIS (= IOVIS) (*D.* 3054N)
> EIOYBIANOS (= IOVIANUS) (*D.* 3170A)

The 18.0 % figure showing the *V* spelling for the intervocalic /u̯/ leaves little doubt that the merger of /b/ and /u̯/ in the intervocalic position was an accomplished fact in Northern Italy during the periods covered by the inscriptions.

(b) *Central*. A high percentage of deviations with respect to the Latin intervocalic /u̯/ is found in the inscriptions from the Central Italian area. Following are examples of deviations from third/fourth-century inscriptions:

> VIBES (*D.* 900), two times in the same inscription
> NOB. (= NOVEMBRES) (*D.* 1494 a. 394/402)

from fifth-century inscriptions:

> NOBENBRIUM (*D.* 304 a. 490)

from sixth/seventh-century inscriptions:

> IUBANTE (*D.* 377 a. 574?)
> ABUNCULO (= AVUNCULO) (*D.* 846 VI cent.)[32]

---

[32] Cf. Fr. *oncle*, Prov. *ouncle*, Roum. *unchiu* < AUVNCULUS; but Sp. *tío*, Sard. *tiu*, It. *zio* < *Lat.* THIUS Gk.

From undated inscriptions, a few examples follow:

>   LABA (= LAVAT) (*D.* 1557)
>   LABES (= LAVAS) (*D.* 3427)
>   ZOBINUS (= IOVINUS) (*D.* 4451B)
>   IUBENTE (= IUVENTE) (*D.* 2012)

Although in Central Italy, the percentage of *V* spelling for intervocalic /b/ (8.3 %) is just about the same as it is in Northern Italy (8.6 %), we were not able to determine, with certainty, the possibility of an intervocalic /b/ - /u̯/ merger in the former area because five out of the eight deviations are found in proper nouns and may be of doubtful significance. On the other hand, the 22.2 % figure showing the *B* for intervocalic /u̯/ clearly indicates that an intervocalic /b/ - /u̯/ merger was an accomplished fact in Central Italy during the periods covered by the inscriptions.

(c) *Southern*. A high percentage (48.9 %) of deviations with respect to the spelling of the Latin intervocalic /u̯/ is also found in the inscriptions from Southern Italy. Following are the examples of deviations from third/fourth-century inscriptions (all examples are from the fourth century):

>   FABENTE (= FAVENTE) (*D.* 97 a. 367)
>   EUBODIO (= EUVODIO) (*D.* 398 a. 386)
>   NOBEN (= NOVEMBRES) (*D.* 1491 a. 392)

from the fifth century:

>   FL[A]B[IUS] (= FLAVIUS) (*D.* 3933B a. 431)
>   FLABIO (*D.* 3114 a. 469)

Some examples from the sixth century are:

>   FABENTE (*D.* 173 a. 583)
>   MABURTI (= MAVURTI) (*D.* 3030 a. 527)
>   VIBUM (= VIVUM) (*D.* 3862 a. 553)
>   OCTABA (= OCTAVA) (*D.* 4677 a. 529)

Some examples from undated inscriptions are:

CIBIS (= CIVIS) (*D.* 1746)
BIBAS (= VIVAS) (*D.* 2195N)
EBENIAT (= EVENIAT) (*D.* 2417N)
RENOBATUS (= RENOVATUS) (*D.* 3445A)
CIBITATI (= CIVITATIS) (*D.* 4893A)

Let us recall that in Southern Italy (as in Central Italy) we were not able to determine the possibility of an intervocalic /b/ - /u̯/ merger on the basis of deviations from the expected *B* (since they are limited to proper nouns).

A similar state of affairs seems to obtain in this area with respect to deviations from the expected *V*, at least in the earlier centuries. It will be observed that in third/fourth-century inscriptions the 50.0 % figure is based on only three occurrences of the expected V and three deviations (one in a proper noun); in fifth-century inscriptions the 20.0 % figure is based on only eight occurrences of the expected *V* and two deviations (both in proper nouns). However, the 38.7 % figure in sixth/seventh-century inscriptions (on the basis of sixteen occurrences of the expected *V* and ten deviations, one in a proper noun) and the 60.0 % figure in undated inscriptions (on the basis of twenty occurrences of the expected *V* and thirty deviations, four in proper nouns (not shown), indicate an intervocalic /b/ - /u̯/ merger in this area. If we leave eight deviations in proper nouns out of our total count, we get a 44.0 % figure. This is also sufficient to indicate an intervocalic /b/ - /u̯/ merger in this area.

2. *Postconsonantal Position*

2.1 CLat. *B* after /l/

Area	Century	(-LB-) → -LB-	(-LB-) → -LV-
Northern	IV/V	1	0
	VI/VII	0	0
	n. d.	4	0
	Totals	5	0
Central	III/IV	0	0
	V	2	0
	VI/VII	0	0
	n. d.	0	0
	Totals	2	0

THE EVOLUTION OF THE LATIN /b/ - /u̯/ MERGER

Area	Century	(-LB-) → -LB-	(-LB-) → -LV-
Southern	III/IV	1	0
	V	0	0
	VI/VII	0	0
	Totals	1	0

(a) *Northern*. There are five occurrences of words with -LB-, and no deviations.

(b) *Central*. There are two occurrences of words with -LB-, and no deviations.

(c) *Southern*. There is only one occurrence of the expected -LB-, and no deviations.

2.2 CLat. *B* after /r/

Area	Century	(-RB-) → -RB-	(-RB-) → -RV-
Northern	IV/V	2	0
	VI/VII	0	0
	n. d.	1	0
	Totals	3	0
Central	III/IV	0	0
	V	0	0
	VI/VII	1	0
	n. d.	0	0
	Totals	1	0
Southern	III/IV	0	0
	V	0	0
	VI/VII	2	0
	n. d.	1	0
	Totals	3	0

(a) *Northern*. There are three occurrences of words with the expected -RB-, and no deviations.

(b) *Central*. There is only one occurrence of the expected -RB-, and no deviations.

(c) *Southern*. There are three words with the expected -RB-. There are no deviations. We did find, however, two instances where an expected -SB- was spelled -SV-. There was one occurrence of the expected -SB- in an undated inscription.

2.4 CLat. V after /l/

Area	Century	(-LV-) → -LV-	(-LV-) → -LB-	%
Northern	IV/V	0	0	
	VI/VII	0	0	
	n. d.	7	4	
	Totals	7	4	36.3
Central	III/IV	0	0	
	V	1	0	
	VI/VII	3	0	
	n. d.	4	0	
	Totals	8	0	0.0
Southern	III/IV	0	0	
	V	0	0	
	VI/VII	2	0	
	n. d.	2	4	
	Totals	4	4	50.0

(a) *Northern*. There are seven cases of words with the expected -*LV*-. The four -*LB*- spellings for -*LV*- are found in undated inscriptions and are the following:

> SOLB. (= SOLVUNT) (*D.* 1890)
> SOLIBUNT (*D.* 1890N)
> SOLBIT (*D.* 488A; *D.* 567)[1]

(b) *Central*. There are eight occurrences of words with the expected -*LV*- spelling, and no deviations.

(c) *Southern*. There are four occurrences of words with the expected -*LV*-. The four examples of the use of -*LB*- for -*LV*- are found in undated inscriptions and are the following:

> SALBO (= SALVO) (*D.* 1009N)
> SILBINA (*D.* 2533)
> SILBESTRO (*D.* 2591)
> SILBIUS (*D.* 3445)

The 50 % figure may be misleading since it is based on a total of only four cases of the expected -*LV*- spelling and four deviations with -*LB*-. Three of these deviations are found in proper nouns where misspellings are more likely to occur. If we leave

112   THE EVOLUTION OF THE LATIN /b/ - /u̯/ MERGER

these three deviations in proper nouns out of our count, we get a 20 % figure based on a single reliable deviation.

2.5 CLat. V after /r/

Area	Century	(-RV-) → -RV-	(-RV-) → -RB-	%
Northern	IV/V	3	0	
	VI/VII	1	0	
	n. d.	3	2	
	Totals	7	2	22.2
Central	III/IV	1	0	
	V	0	0	
	VI/VII	5	1	
	n. d.	5	2	
	Totals	11	3	21.3
Southern	III/IV	0	0	
	V	1	0	
	VI/VII	2	0	
	n. d.	3	2	
	Totals	6	2	25.0

(a) *Northern*. There are seven words with the expected -*RV*-. The two examples of the use of -*RB*- for -*RV*- are found in undated inscriptions. They are:

SERBUS (*D.* 560)
CERBONIAE (*D.* 3442), a proper noun

(b) *Central*. There are eleven occurrences of words with -*RV*-. Although there are no examples of -*LB*- for -*LV*-, there are three examples of -*RB*- for -*RV*-. The only deviation in dated inscriptions occurs in the sixth century in the form

SERBAVIT (*D.* 1005 a. 570)

In undated inscriptions -*RB*- for -*RV*- occurs twice in the form

SERBUS (*D.* 257N; *D.* 1455A)

(c) *Southern*. There are six occurrences of words with -*RV*-. The two -*RB*- spellings for -*RV*- are found in undated inscriptions. They are:

SERBULUS (D. 1297A)
PARBULUS (D. 3980)

In undated inscriptions from this area, there are also four occurrences of words with the expected -DV- (/du̯/). There is one example, in an undated inscription, of the use of -DB- for -DV- in the proper noun QUOBULDEO (D. 3137A), for an expected QUODVULTDEUS.

2.6 SUMMARY: *The B-V Alternation in Postconsonantal Position*

It would be well to summarize our data concerning the B and V spelling in postconsonantal position to see if we can learn anything about the status of the Latin /b/ and /u̯/ in this position. All deviations (except one from Central Italy) are found in undated inscriptions; hence the absence of a tabular breakdown of our data according to centuries. (In the heading, the capital C stands for *Consonant*.) The summary table of total correct occurrences and deviations is as follows:

Area	(-CB-) → -CV-		%	(-CV-) → -CB-		%
Northern	8	0	0.0	14	6	30.0
Central	3	0	0.0	19	3	13.6
Southern	5	2	28.5	14	7	33.3

(a) *Northern*. There are eight cases of the B in postconsonantal position and no deviations with V. It would be difficult to make any definite statement concerning the stability of the /b/ on the basis of such a scanty sampling. Can the 30 % figure (26.3 %, if we leave one deviation in a proper noun out of our count) be taken as evidence of a strengthening of the Latin /u̯/ in postconsonantal position in the direction of a bilabial fricative?

(b) *Central*. It would be difficult to make any statement concerning the stability of the Latin /b/ in this position on the basis of only three occurrences of this consonant in this area, a rather scanty sampling. Can the 13.6 % figure be taken as evidence of a strengthening of the Latin postconsonantal /u̯/? Perhaps so, but we must also remember that the 13.0 % figure is based on only three deviations in this position.

(c) *Southern*. Although the 28.5 % figure is based on only five correct cases of the postconsonantal B and two deviations with V, it may have some importance in the light of the even higher percentage of B spellings for V in this position (33.3 % based on fourteen cases of the V and seven deviations with B). This percentage figure is reduced to 17.6 % if we leave out four deviations in proper nouns. Taken together, both figures indicate that this spelling alternation has its source in some kind of phonological change — perhaps an incipient postconsonantal /b/ - /u̯/ merger.

3. *Verb Endings*

3.1 CLat. B /b/ in Future Tense Endings, e.g., DA-BIT → DA-VIT

Latin /b/ in the third person singular, future indicative active, is shown in the following table. It will be observed that, with one exception,[33] the occurrence of this tense ending is limited to the Northern Italian area. We give the ratio of correct occurrences and deviations:

Area	Century	(-BIT) → -BIT	(-BIT) → -VIT	%
Northern	IV/V	19	9	32.1
	VI/VII	0	0	
	n. d.	0	1	
	Totals	19	10	34.4

The use of V for B in this tense ending in Northern Italy is limited to the verb form DABIT. With one exception, all deviations are found on fourth/fifth-century inscriptions (none of which is specifically dated) from the *Concordia* military cemetery. The form DAVIT for DABIT occurs on the following dated inscriptions: (D. 370; D. 436; D. 494; D. 524; D. 544; D. 555; D. 556; D. 716; and D. 812). The only example of -VIT for -BIT in undated inscriptions is in the expression DAVIT IN FESCU ET SOLE (D. 2216).

---

[33] The only other occurrence of the future tense in these Italian regions is on an undated inscription from Southern Italy, which reads: ANIMAS CHRISTUS REVOCABIT IN UNUM (D. 3478).

In his study of the language of a collection of eighth-century documents from Northern Italy,[34] R. L. Politzer cites one example of the use of V for B in the third person singular future tense in the expression *vitam hedernam possedevit* (= *vitam aeternam possedebit*) and draws attention to its "identity with perfect."

3.2 CLat. V /u/ in Perfect Tense Endings of REQUIE-VIT → REQUIE-BIT, and in the Perfect Tense of Other Verbs

In this section, data concerning the Latin V are restricted to the third person singular perfect tense ending of REQUIESCERE and of other verbs.

Area	Century	(-VIT) → VIT	(-VIT) → BIT	%
Northern	IV/V	15	2	13.3
	VI/VII	2	1	(33.3)
	n. d.	10	3	23.1
	Totals	27	6	18.1
Central	III/IV	0	1	
	V	3	0	
	VI/VII	9	1	
	n. d.	5	1	
	Totals	17	3	15.0
Southern	III/IV	1	1	(50.0)
	V	1	3	75.0
	VI/VII	0	2	100.0
	n. d.	11	17	60.7
	Totals	13	23	63.8

(a) *Northern.* In dated inscriptions the *-BIT* spelling for *-VIT* appears in the following forms:

> COMPARABIT (= COMPARAVIT) (*D.* 472 ca. V cent.)
> MILITABIT (*D.* 515 IV/V cent.)
> FUNDABIT (*D.* 749 a. 546)

In undated inscriptions the *B* for *V* in this perfect tense ending occurs in the following forms:

---

[34] R. L. Politzer, *A Study of the Language of the Eighth-Century Lombardic Documents* (New York, 1949), p. 116.

116   THE EVOLUTION OF THE LATIN /b/ - /ṷ/ MERGER

>PAUSABIT (*D.* 1364; *D.* 3240)
>PRECABIT (= PRAECAVIT) (*D.* 4365)

Northern Italy is the only Italian area which shows an absence of *B* spellings for *V* in the verb form REQUIESCERE.

(b) *Central.* In dated inscriptions, deviations are found in the following forms; from third/fourth-century inscriptions:

>AEDIFICABIT (*D.* 3827 a. 361)
>RENOVABIT (*D.* 261 a. 573/574)

In undated inscriptions we found the form REQUIEBIT (*D.* 1153).

(c) *Southern.* Deviations include the following forms, from third/fourth-century inscriptions:

>REQUIEBIT (*D.* 2883Na a. 380)

from fifth-century inscriptions:

>CURABIT (*D.* 1026 VII cent.)
>QUIEBIT (= REQUIEVIT), and NOBABIT (= NOVAVIT), both on the same inscription (*D.* 1091 ca. V cent.)

from sixth/seventh-century inscriptions:

>RENOVABIT (*D.* 261 a. 573/574)

In undated inscriptions from Southern Italy, thirteen out of seventeen deviations occur in the verb form REQUIEVIT, which appears variously spelled as REQUIEBIT (*D.* 2734N), QUIEBIT (*D.* 3063Aa), and QUIBIT (*D.* 3103c), etc. The remaining four deviations occur in

>MILITABIT (*D.* 569)
>CONFORTABIT (*D.* 1790)
>RENOVABIT (*D.* 1902D)
>CUNPARAB[IT] (= COMPARAVIT) (*D.* 3759A)

3.3 *CLat.* V /u̯/ *in other verb endings*

The expected *V* occurs sporadically in the first person singular/third-person plural, perfect active indicative endings, and in the third person singular, future perfect active indicative/perfect active subjunctive ending (both are represented in Classical Latin by one and the same form, namely, *-VERIT*). The following table shows occurrences of these endings and the deviations (which occur in dated and undated inscriptions from the Northern and Southern areas only) found in our inscriptions:

3.3a CLat. V /μ/ in other verb endings

A. first person singular perfect active indicative
B. third person plural perfect active indicative
C. third person singular future perfect active indicative/ perfect active subjunctive

Area	Century	A (-VI)→-BI	%	B (-VERUNT)→ BERUNT	%	C (-VERIT)→ BERIT	%	Tot. Cor.	Tot. Dev.	%
Northern	IV/V	1		6		3		10	0	
	VI/VII	0		0	0	0		0	0	
	n. d.	1		0	1	0		1	1	
	Totals	2	0	6	1	(14.3)	3	0	11	1	
Central	III/IV	0		1	0	0		1	0	
	V	0		0	0	2	0	0	4	0	
	VI/VII	1		1	0	0		1	0	
	n. d.	0		0	0	1	0	1	0	
	Totals	1	0	2	0		3	0	6	0	
Southern	III/IV	0		0	0	0		0	0	
	V	0		0	1	0		0	1	
	VI/VII	0		1	2	0		1	2	66.6
	n. d.	1		1	0	1		3	1	
	Totals	1	0	2	3	60.0	1	1	(50.0)	4	4	50.0

3.3b *CLat. V /u̯/ in other verb endings*

As can be seen from the preceding table, occurrences of the Latin /u̯/ in other verb endings are infrequent and deviations are limited to the third person plural perfect active indicative and the third person singular future perfect active indicative/perfect active subjunctive endings. Following are the examples:

(a) *First Person Singular Perfect Active Indicative.*

There are only two occurrences of this particular ending and no deviations.

(b) *Third Person Plural Perfect Active Indicative.*

The *B* spelling for *V* in this ending occurs on inscriptions from Northern and Southern Italian areas only.

(1) *Northern.* Out of a total of eight possible cases of the expected *V*, one is spelled with *B* on an undated inscription and reads:

> PROBABERUNT (*D.* 1933)

(2) *Southern.* There are two cases of the expected *V*, one in an undated inscription, and three deviations with *B* found on dated inscriptions. These deviations are:

> CONPA[RA]BER[U]NT (= COMPARAVERUNT)
> (*D.* 3735 ca. V cent.)
> CONPARABERUNT AND COMMENDABERNU
> (= COMMENDAVERUNT), both on the same seventh-century inscription (*D.* 3860 a. 612).

(c) *Third Person Singular Future Perfect Indicative Active/ Perfect Subjunctive Active.*

There is only one instance of a *B* spelling for Latin /u̯/ in these verb endings in our entire inscriptional material. It is found on an undated inscription from Southern Italy and reads:

> APERBERIT (= APERAVERIT) (*D.* 825)

3.4 SUMMARY: *The Latin V in All Perfect Tense Endings and Other Verb Endings Together*

Data concerning Latin V /u̯/ in these verb endings are shown in the following table. The purpose of this table is twofold:

(a) to show deviations from the expected V, and

(b) to summarize the data concerning the use of B to represent /u̯/ in these verb endings as contributory evidence of a merger of /b/ and /u̯/ in the intervocalic position in Italy.

Our criteria in this connection will be the total number of correct occurrences of the V in these verb endings and deviations therefrom. The ratio of correct occurrences and deviations in Northern, Central, and Southern Italy is as follows:

Area	Century	(V) → B		%
Northern	IV/V	25	2	7.4
	VI/VII	2	1	(33.3)
	n. d.	11	4	20.7
	Totals	38	7	15.6
Central	III/IV	1	1	(100.0)
	V	3	0	0.0
	VI/VII	13	1	(7.1)
	n. d.	6	1	(14.2)
	Totals	23	3	11.5
Southern	III/IV	1	1	(100.0)
	V	1	4	80.0
	VI/VII	1	4	80.0
	n. d.	14	18	56.3
	Totals	17	27	61.4

(a) *Northern.* The 15.6 % figure based on thirty-eight correct occurrences of the V and seven deviations with B permits us to conclude that an intervocalic /b/ - /u̯/ merger took place in Northern Italy during the periods covered by the inscriptions.

(b) *Central.* The absence of a consistent pattern of deviations in dated and undated inscriptions, as can be seen in our table, and percentage figures based on single deviations do not permit us to draw any specific conclusion concerning the possibility of an intervocalic /b/ - /u̯/ merger in this area. They can be used as contributory evidence of such a merger in Central Italy.

(c) *Southern*. With the exception of our data in third/fourth-century inscriptions (where there is only one correct case of the expected *V* and one deviation), deviations in inscriptions from later centuries and in undated inscriptions outnumber the correct forms. There is little doubt that of the three Italian areas, Southern Italy is least conservative in its treatment of the expected *V* spelling in verb endings. The conclusion that the 61.4 % figure, on the basis of twenty-seven deviations as against seventeen correct classical spellings, represents a Latin intervocalic /b/ - /u̯/ merger seems justified.

4. Initial Position

4.1 CLat. B /b/

Area	Century	(B) → B	(B) → V	%
Northern	IV/V	34	0	
	VI/VII	13	0	
	n. d.	54	0	
	Totals	101	0	
Central	III/IV	20	0	0.0
	V	3	0	0.0
	VI/VII	19	1	(5.0)
	n. d.	41	2	4.6
	Totals	83	3	3.4
Southern	III/IV	6	0	
	V	9	0	
	VI/VII	35	0	
	n. d.	77	4	4.9
	Totals	127	4	3.1

(a) *Northern*. In the inscriptions from Northern Italy, there are no examples of the use of the letter *V* for initial *B*. On the basis of 101 occurrences of the expected initial *B* and no deviations, we would be justified in stating that the Latin /b/ was pronounced /b/ in initial position.

(b) *Central*. There are a total of eighty-three occurrences of the expected initial *B* and three deviations (or 3.4 %) with *V* in our corpus of inscriptions from Central Italy. The examples of deviations are, from sixth/seventh-century inscriptions:

VASE (= BASE) (*D*. 225 VI cent.)

from undated inscriptions:

VONIFATIA (= BONIFATIA) (*D*. 1602B)
VENE (= BENE) (*D*. 4426B)

The 5.0 % figure in sixth/seventh-century inscriptions may be misleading, since it is based on a single deviation, and, hence, may represent the orthography of a single stonemason. The 4.6 % figure in undated inscriptions may not represent the state of affairs, since it includes one deviation in a proper noun. If we leave this misspelling out of our count, we get a 2.3 % figure based on only a single reliable deviation. On the basis of eighty-three occurrences of the expected initial *B* spelling and only two reliable deviations (or 2.0 %) with *V*, we conclude that the Latin /b/ was quite stable in this position in Central Italy.

(c) *Southern*. There are 127 occurrences of the expected initial *B* spelling and four deviations (or 3.1 %) with *V*. These occur in undated inscriptions and are limited to the form BENE (MERENTI) and read VENE(MERENTI) (*D*. 753N; *D*. 1149; *D*. 2591N; *D*. 2598). Data concerning the Latin *B* /b/ in initial position in Southern Italy seem to show that this consonant was fairly stable during the periods covered by our inscriptions, although the four *V* spellings for initial *B* may have some importance in the light of subsequent phonological developments in this area (cf. *infra*, Sec. 5.2c).

4.2 CLat. *V* /u̯/

Area	Century	(V) → V	(V) → B	%
Northern	IV/V	169	0	
	VI/VII	66	0	
	n. d.	255	20	8.2
	Totals	490	20	3.9

THE B-V ALTERNATION IN LATIN INSCRIPTIONS 123

Area	Century	(V) → V	(V) → B	%
Central	III/IV	45	0	0.0
	V	29	1	(3.3)
	VI/VII	44	1	(2.2)
	n. d.	140	9	6.0
	Totals	258	11	4.0
Southern	III/IV	34	3	8.1
	V	40	1	(2.4)
	VI/VII	62	9	12.6
	n. d.	92	83	47.4
	Totals	228	96	29.6

(a) *Northern*. There are a total of 490 occurrences of the expected *V* spelling and twenty deviations (or 3.9 %) with *B*. Data concerning the use of *B* for initial *V* in the inscriptions from Northern Italy show that this spelling is not so infrequent as the percentage of deviation seems to indicate. This, however, may not be surprising if one keeps in mind the large number of occurrences (a total of 256) of the expected *V* in the stereotyped verb form VIXIT, which one would expect to be least likely to be misspelled. The following examples, all from undated inscriptions, show a *B* spelling for initial *V*:

BIR[G]INI[O] (*D.* 463; *D.* 398; *D.* 4252)
BETRANUS (= VETERANUS) (*D.* 463) [35]
BIXIT (10 times) (*D.* 560; *D.* 1360AN), etc.
BOTU[M] (= VOTUM) (*D.* 1933; *D.* 2745AN; *D.* 4252)
BALBERIO (= VALERIO) (*D.* 1332)
BIBA, -O (= VIVA, -O) (*D.* 2287A; *D.* 3632)

Deviations from the expected spelling of the initial /u̯/ *(V)* amount to 3.9 %. This is below our five percent control figure and is taken as evidence that the initial Latin /u̯/ was stable in Northern Italy and remained distinct from the initial /b/.

(b) *Central*. In the inscriptions from Central Italy, we found a total of 258 occurrences of the expected initial *V* and eleven

---

[35] In connection with this form, Väänänen, *Introduction au latin vulgaire* (Paris: Klincksieck, 1967), p. 41, writes the following: "fréquent dans les inscriptions depuis les 1er s. ap. J.-C.; roum. *batrîn*, it. dial. *vetrano*, frioul. *vedran*.

deviations (or 4.0 %) with B. The examples of B spellings to represent Latin initial /u̯/ are, from the fifth century:

>   CUM BIRGINIUM (= CUM VIRGINIO) (D. 2258 a. 406)

from sixth/seventh-century inscriptions:

>   BIXID (= VIXIT) (D. 1029N ca. VI/VII cent.)

In undated inscriptions, six out of nine deviations occur in the form BIXIT for VIXIT (D. 2450A; D. 2616; D. 2706B; D. 2983AN; D. 4141B; D. 4178). The three remaining examples all occur in proper nouns. They are:

>   BELENTIA (= VALENTIA) (D. 2582)
>   BITTALIAE (= VITALIAE) (D. 4350A)
>   BALERIO (= VALERIO) (D. 4630)

If we leave three deviations in proper nouns out of our total count, the over-all 4.0 % figure is reduced to 3.0 %. Both figures are under the five percent control figure and thus are taken as evidence of stability of the Latin initial /u̯/.

(c) *Southern.* A high percentage of deviations (22.6 %, based on 328 occurrences of the expected initial V and 96 deviations with B) occurs in the inscriptions from Southern Italy. Examples of the use of B for initial V are, from third/fourth-century inscriptions:

>   BISIT (D. 2883Na a. 380)
>   BIXIT (D. 2958 a. 399)
>   BISSIT (D. 3119 a. 389)

In a garbled inscription from the fifth century we found:

>   DEFUNTA [PAU]LINA QUE BISENTS AN[N]OS (D. 2801 (= DEFUNCTA EST PAULINA QUAE VIXIT ANNOS) (a. 408)

In sixth/seventh-century inscriptions we found:

HONESTA BIRCO (= VIRGO) QUI BIXIT (= VIXIT) (*D*. 341a a. 553)
B. (= VIXIT) (*D*. 341b a. 553)
BISSIT (= VIXIT) (*D*. 3549 a. 570)
BUSSI (= VIXIT) (*D*. 3851 VII cent.)
BIOLARI (= VIOLARET) (*D*. 3868 a. 527)
BIXIT (*D*. 4584 a. 570)
BIRO (= VIRO), BIXET, on the same inscription (*D*. 4677 a. 529)

The data culled from undated inscriptions from this area indeed supplement those found in dated inscriptions. Following are some of the eighty-three examples of the use of *B* for initial *V:*

BICARIUS (= VICARIUS) (*D*. 580)
BIRGO (= VIRGO) (*D*. 1353A)
BICXI (= VIXIT) (*D*. 2932A)
BIGINTI (= VIGINTI) (*D*. 3350)
BOLUERIT (= VOLUERIT) (*D*. 3858N)
BENUS (= VENUS) (*D*. 4904)

If we leave seventeen deviations in proper nouns out of our count, the 47.4 % figure in undated inscriptions, and the 29.6 % overall figure are reduced to 41.8 % and 19.4 % respectively. It is not unreasonable to interpret these figures (well over the five percent control figure) as evidence of a complete merger of the Latin /b/ and /u̯/ in initial position in the Vulgar Latin of Southern Italy.

5. *Summary and Conclusions*

We may now summarize our data concerning the treatment of Latin /b/ and /u̯/ in the interior position in Italy, taking the total number of occurrences of these consonants and the total number of orthographic deviations from their expected spelling. To the extent that our data permit us, we will also attempt to make general statements regarding possible regional chronological developments. We find the following percentage figures for each of the three Italian areas under study:

5a Comparative Tables Concerning the Treatment of the Latin /b/ and /u̯/ in the Interior Position

Area	Century	(B) → V		%	(V) → B		%
Northern	IV/V	61	15	19.7	58	3	4.9
	VI/VII	10	0	0.0	23	4	14.8
	n. d.	41	3	6.8	53	24	31.1
	Totals	112	18	13.8	134	31	18.7
Central	III/IV	19	3	13.6	7	6	46.1
	V	14	1	(6.7)	11	1	8.3
	VI/VII	8	1	(11.1)	28	4	12.5
	n. d.	39	3	7.1	52	11	17.5
	Totals	80	8	9.1	98	22	18.3
Southern	III/IV	13	0	0.0	4	4	50.0
	V	6	1	(14.3)	10	6	37.5
	VI/VII	16	2	11.1	21	14	40.0
	n. d.	53	2	3.6	43	55	56.1
	Totals	88	5	5.4	78	79	50.3

5.1 SUMMARY: *The Latin /b/ and /u̯/ in the Interior Position*

(a) *Northern.* In fourth/fifth-century inscriptions from this area we find that the percentage of deviation from the expected interior *V* is about one-fifth the percentage of deviation from the expected interior *B* in approximately the same amount of material. We get a 4.9 % incidence of *B* to represent original interior /u̯/ (fifty-eight cases of the expected *V* and three examples with B), compared with a 19.7 % incidence of *V* to represent original interior /b/ (sixty-one cases of the expected *B* and fifteen examples with *V*). The high frequency of the use of *V* for the expected interior *B*, together with the three examples showing the use of *B* for interior *V*, in the earliest Christian inscriptions from Northern Italy is good evidence of a merger of Latin intervocalic /b/ and /u̯/ by this time. Is the contrast between these data from Northern Italy of the early centuries and the data from other regions of the same time to be explained as due to regional differences? Another question is raised by the absence of *V* spellings for interior *B* in the sixth and seventh centuries, in contrast to the frequent spellings with *V* in the fourth and fifth centuries. A third question is raised by the frequent use of *V* for interior *B* in the eighth-century documents from Northern Italy (*infra*, p. 151). The fact that there is a total of only ten occurrences of the interior /b/ in the later two centuries, i.e., one-sixth the number of occurrences of this consonant with respect to the previous two centuries, may be offered as a possible explanation for the absence of deviations in our corpus. On the other hand, during this same period we observe a 10 % differential showing B for original /u̯/ over the early centuries (from 4.9 % in fourth/fifth-century inscriptions to 14.8 % in sixth/seventh-century inscriptions). Whatever the reasons for the skewing, now in favor of deviations from the expected interior B, now in favor of those from the expected interior V, may be, the number of instances in which the original Latin /b/ and /u̯/ are misspelled V and B respectively in dated and undated inscriptions, i.e., the over-all 13.8 % use of V for B and the over-all 18.7 % use of B for V, leave little doubt that an intervocalic /b/ - /u̯/ merger was an accomplished fact by the time of the appearance of our Christian Latin inscriptions from Northern Italy. If we leave a total of four deviations from the expected interior V in proper nouns out of our count (one in sixth/seventh-century inscriptions, and three in undated inscriptions), we get a 16.8 % figure. This is still conclusive as to an intervocalic /b/ - /u̯/ merger.

In Northern Italy, as in Lugdunensis, we wondered whether there was any connection between a possible early voicing of Latin intervocalic /-p-/ > /-b-/ and the lower frequency of B for original /u̯/ in the time of the early inscriptions from Northern Italy. We investigated this possibility. In fourth/fifth-century inscriptional material we found seventy-six cases of the expected intervocalic -P- spelling and no deviations with B; in sixth/seventh-century inscriptions there were twenty-one occurrences of the expected intervocalic -P- spelling and no deviations with -B-; in undated inscriptions we found thirty-one occurrences of the expected intervocalic -P- spelling and no deviations with -B-. Evidence of stability of the Latin intervocalic /p/ in dated inscriptions up to the first quarter of the seventh century in Northern Italy means an absence of voicing of the Latin intervocalic /-p-/ to /-b-/.

Voicing of the Latin intervocalic /p/ to /b/ seems to have taken place in Northern Italy in the eighth century. We cannot say how much earlier than this a voicing of intervocalic /-p-/ > /-b-/ had actually begun. In his study of the eighth-century *Codice Paleo-*

grafico Lombardo, R. L. Politzer gives quantitative data concerning the use of *B* to represent the Latin intervocalic /p/. He records seventy-five occurrences of the expected intervocalic *-P-* spelling and nine deviations (or 10.7 %) with *-B-*. He concludes: "The documents show the voicing of intervocalic $p > b$" (p. 51). Politzer also gives *(ibid.)* one example of the use of the letter *-v-* where the original Latin form had a *-p-*. This occurs in the form *savere* < SAPERE. On the basis of this example, Politzer believes that at this time the /-b-/ resulting from a voicing of the Latin voiceless intervocalic /-p-/ became /b/ or /v/. He writes thus: "The sound (i.e., /-p-/) after changing to *b* (i.e., /-b-/) could also take part in the fluctuating pronunciation of the *b* sound."

In the eighth-century *Codice Diplomatico Longobardo,*[36] a collection of Latin documents from North Italian regions north of the Spezia-Rimini line, written from approximately 720 to 744, R. L. Politzer cites evidence to support his belief that a general voicing of the Latin intervocalic /p, t, k/ took place in the eighth century. A possible early voicing of Latin intervocalic /-p-/ to /-b-/ might have been a factor contributing to the lower frequency of *B* for original /u̯/ in the time of the early inscriptions from Northern Italy, but a consideration of data from our inscriptions and those given by Politzer do not lend support to this possibility.

A closer examination shows that nine out of the fifteen examples of *V* for intervocalic *B* in the early North Italian inscriptions are in the verb form DAVIT (= DABIT) (Sec. 3.1), which appears in a stereotyped formula. These spellings are all found in the same place, viz. the *Concordia* military cemetery, and may represent localisms only.

In his study of the language of eighth-century Latin documents from Northern Italy, Robert Politzer points out *(Documents,* p. 51) that "The spelling *v* for intervocalic *b* occurs frequently in our texts." He counts 265 cases of the expected intervocalic *b* spelling and seventy-three deviations (or 21.5 %) with *v*. He does not give quantitative data concerning the use of *b* for intervocalic *v*. The contrast between our data and those of Politzer on the intervocalic /b/ - /u̯/ merger in Northern Italy may be due

---

[36] "A Note on the North Italian Voicing of Intervocalic Stops," *Word,* XI (1955), 416-419.

to the fact that stonemasons and scribes had very different training and professional traditions. Politzer sums up his conclusions regarding the intervocalic /b/ - /u̯/ merger in Northern Italy thus (p. 51):

> Many documents ... some of them in the early part of the century — show the change with such high relative frequency that it is safe to assume that we are dealing with a phonologically established phenomenon, ...

(b) *Central*. The absence of a consistent pattern of deviations from the expected *B* spelling makes it difficult for us to make a general statement regarding the stability of the Latin intervocalic /b/ in Central Italy. Through the fifth century, the *V* spellings for interior *B* occur in proper nouns only, which generally lend themselves to more frequent misspellings than do common words used in daily communication. So, then, it is doubtful whether the 13.6 % figure in third/fourth-century inscriptions and the 6.7 % figure in fifth-century inscriptions represent the state of affairs. The 11.1 % figure in sixth/seventh-century inscriptions may be misleading, since it is based on a single deviation only. If we leave one misspelling in a proper noun out of our count, the 7.1 % figure in undated inscriptions is reduced to 4.8 %. The 9.1 % over-all figure may be misleading, since it includes five deviations in proper nouns. The resulting 5.8 % figure, then, is based on only three reliable deviations. These are too few, it would seem, to permit us to speak of anything more than a possible trend towards an intervocalic /b/ - /u̯/ merger in this area. We must turn to our data concerning the use of *B* to represent interior /u̯/ to see if the inscriptions give us any indication of such a merger.

The figures presented in the table show a low reliability in representing the Latin interior /u̯/. The 46.1 % figure in the third/fourth-century inscriptions is based on a total of only thirteen possible occurrences of the interior /u̯/ (a rather small sampling). This figure is reduced to 41.6 %, since it includes one *B* spelling for *V* in a proper noun. Despite the scanty sampling of material, it would not be unreasonable to think that a Latin intervocalic /b/ - /u̯/ merger was well under-way in Central Italy by this time. The 8.3 % figure in fifth-century inscriptions may be misleading, since it is based on a single deviation. This may represent the error of a single stonemason. There is no reason to think, however, that such a widespread phenomenon in Vulgar Latin should not have been as advanced at this time in Central Italy as it appears to have been in the preceding and later centuries. The frequency of occurrence of *B* as a misspelling for /u̯/ in undated inscriptions (17.5 %) and the 18.3 % figure over-all leave little doubt that an intervocalic /b/ - /u̯/ merger was an accomplished fact in Central Italy during the periods covered by our inscriptions. If we leave a total of four deviations in proper nouns out of our count (one in third/fourth-century inscriptions, mentioned above, and three in undated inscriptions), we get a 15.5 % over-all figure based on eighteen reliable deviations. This high percentage figure is conclusive as to an intervocalic /b/ - /u̯/ merger.

A contrast in the data on the intervocalic /b/ - /u̯/ merger is well illustrated by a comparison of our inscriptions with a study of eighth-century Latin documents from Central Italy by Elizabeth M. Goff.[37] In her documents (as in Politzer's), she finds that data showing an inconsistency in the use of interior *B* and *V* are skewed in favor of deviations from the expected *B*. She writes thus: "The substitution of *b* for *v* is much less frequent than that of *v* for *b*" (p. 81). She finds 292 cases of the expected intervocalic *b* and 205 instances (or 41.2 %) with *v*. On the other hand, she points out that "a limited number of examples of *b* for *v* are to be found in the documents" (p. 25). She finds 118 cases of the expected intervocalic *v* and eleven deviations (or 8.5 %) with *b*. The contrast between our data and those of Goff on the intervocalic /b/ - /u̯/ merger in Central Italy may be due to the fact that stonemasons and scribes had very different training and professional traditions. Goff sums up her conclusions on the intervocalic /b/ - /u̯/ merger thus:

> The two letters doubtless represent a single sound, the nature of which was probably the bilabial spirant, an intermediate stage between the /b/ and the /w/ of classical Latin and the /v/ of Romance (p. 81).

---

[37] Elizabeth Mary Goff, "The Language of the Eighth-Century Documents in Central Italy" (unpublished Ph.D. Dissertation, Department of French and Romance Philology, Columbia University, 1958).

(c) *Southern*. In Southern Italy, as in Central Italy, an absence of a consistent pattern of deviations from the expected interior *B* spelling in dated and undated inscriptions does not permit us to draw any general conclusion regarding the stability of the Latin intervocalic /b/. In third/fourth-century inscriptions we found thirteen occurrences of the interior *B* and no deviations with *V*. The 14.3 % figure in fifth century inscriptions may be misleading, since there was a total of only six cases of the expected interior *B* and one deviation with *V*. This may represent the error of a single stonemason. The 11.1 % figure in sixth/seventh-century inscriptions may not represent the state of affairs either, since it is based entirely on two deviations found in proper nouns. Consequently, this figure could easily be reduced to 0.0 %. The 3.6 % figure based on only two deviations in undated inscriptions is reduced to 1.8 %, since it includes one *V* spelling for *B* in a proper noun. It seems that figures representing deviations from the expected *B* spelling in dated and undated inscriptions are either negligible or of doubtful significance. It is doubtful, then, whether the 5.4 % over-all figure represents the state of affairs, since it includes a total of three deviations in proper nouns. The resulting 2.2 % over-all figure, based on only two reliable deviations, is not sufficient to permit us to draw any specific conclusion regarding a possible Latin intervocalic /b/ - /u̯/ merger.

It would be difficult to determine the possibility of the existence of such a merger if it were not for the numerous examples of *B* spellings for *V* which, of course, are evidence of such a phenomenon. We now turn to our data concerning the use of *B* to represent Latin interior /u̯/.

It is obvious from the table that in dated and undated inscriptions the interior /u̯/ is represented by *B* with a significantly higher frequency than is the case of interior /b̯/ represented by *V*. The 50.0 % figure in third/fourth-century inscriptions and the consistently high percentage of deviation in the later centuries (37.5 % in the fifth century and 40.0 % during the sixth/seventh-centuries), coupled with a 56.1 % figure in undated inscriptions and a 50.3 % figure over-all, clearly indicate that a Latin intervocalic /b/ - /u̯/ merger was an accomplished fact in Southern Italy during the periods covered by our inscriptions. If we leave a total of twelve deviations in proper nouns out of our count (one in third/fourth-century inscriptions, two in the fifth century, one in sixth/seventh-century inscriptions, and eight in undated ones), we get a 46.2 % over-all figure based on sixty-seven reliable deviations. This is also conclusive as to intervocalic /b/ - /u̯/ merger.

When we compare the results of our findings with those of a study of pagan inscriptions from Pompeii undertaken by V. Väänänen,[38] we find a marked contrast between the two sets of data. He analyzes (pp. 86-88) a number of examples showing an inconsistency in the use of the *B* and the *V* and accounts for them in various ways, like assimilation, dissimilation, uncertain reading ("leçon plus ou moins douteuse"), or uncertain interpretation ("diverses interprétations"). In two instances he claims that the use of *B* for *V* is probably a result of a transliteration of Greek *beta*. Whatever the reasons for the inconsistency in the use of *B* and *V* may be, the conclusion reached by Väänänen is of interest to us from the point of view of regional differences. Indeed this scholar finds that "Très peu nombreux et douteux sont les cas de confusion entre *u* consonne et *b*" (p. 216). Could the contrast between our data and those of Väänänen on the intervocalic /b/ - /u̯/ merger be explained as due to regional differences? Possibly so, since his data are based on inscriptions from one region only, viz. Pompeii. On the other hand, if his data are of doubtful significance, as they seem to be, this may be due to the fact that the bulk of his inscriptions are of an extremely early date (Pompeii was destroyed by the eruption of Vesuvius in 79 A. D.), and a possible intervocalic /b/ - /u̯/ merger may have been only in its beginning stages in this area. No documents in the vernacular from Southern Italy are available before the middle of the tenth century (*infra*, Sec. 5.2c).

5.2 SUMMARY: *The Latin /b/ and /u̯/ in the Initial Position*

(a) *Northern*. In the inscriptions from Northern Italy, the Latin initial /b/ is universally spelled *B*, a state of affairs which parallels that observed in Gaul. The low frequency of deviations from the expected initial *V* spelling (3.9 %) leads us to conclude that the Latin initial /u̯/ was stable in Northern Italy. Evidence

---

[38] V. Väänänen, *Le Latin vulgaire des inscriptions pompéiennes*.

of stability of the initial /b/ and /u̯/ means a conservation of the phonemic distinction.

R. L. Politzer *(Documents)* makes no mention of a *b-v* alternation in initial position in this eighth-century Latin documents from Northern Italy. By his silence on the subject, he leads us to infer that the Latin /b/ and /u̯/ remained distinct in initial position.

(b) *Central.* The infrequency of V spellings for initial B and vice versa (3.4 % and 4.0 %, respectively) is taken as evidence that the Latin initial /b/ and /u̯/ remained distinct in initial position.

In her study of a number of eighth-century Latin documents from Central Italy, E. M. Goff (*op. cit.*, p. 26) records fourteen examples of the use of *b* for initial *v*. She does not give the number of cases of the expected initial *v* spelling, nor does she give quantitative data on the use of *v* for initial *b* in her documents. By her silence on the subject, she leads us to infer that the Latin /b/ and /u̯/ remained distinct in initial position in Central Italy.

(c) *Southern.* The low reliability in representing the Latin initial /u̯/ (22.6 % deviation from the expected initial V spelling), taken together with the 3.1 % use of V for initial B is interpreted as evidence of a Latin /b/ /u̯/ merger in initial position. The possibility of an Oscan substratum influence upon the phonological development of Southern Italy has been advanced to account for the merger of initial /b/ and /u̯/.[39]

Evidence from the earliest documents in Romance from Southern Italy seems to indicate a continuation of the existence of a merger of initial /b/ and /u̯/ already begun in Vulgar Latin. In the *Placito Capuano* (a. 960), from the Benedictine monastery of Monte Cassino, we read forms and expressions like *super ipsa billa* (= *super ipsa villa*), *bolendo* (= *volendo*), *ante nos benire fecimus* (= *ante nos venire fecimus*). In the *Ritmo Cassinese* (twelfth century) from the region of Fondi (on the border of Latium

---

[39] A. Terraccini, "Di che cosa fanno la storia gli storici dei linguaggio? Storia dei tipi *Benio* e *Nerba* nel latino volgare," *Acta Glottologico Italiano*, 27 (1935), 133-152; 28 (1936), 1-31, 134-150. Cf. also R. L. Politzer, "On *b* and *v* in Latin and Romance," where this scholar speaks of Greek influence in this area.

and Campania) we read forms and expressions like *lo bostru audire* (= *lo vostro audire*), *de questa bita* (= *de questa vita*), *lo bollo* (= *lo voglio*), *bengo* (= *vengo*), *de ssa bostra* (= *vostra*) *dignitate*, *de bedere* (= *vedere*).[40]

C. H. Grandgent already raises the question of a possible chronology of the intervocalic /b/ - /u̯/ merger in Italy when he writes: "The development probably began in the first century, was well along in the second, and was completed, at least in Italy, in the third."[41] The comparative findings in our inscriptions seems to permit the possibility of a more precise chronological analysis. On the basis of some specifically dated inscriptions, Grandgent's genralization would seem to need modification to the effect that (1) an intervocalic /b/ - /u̯/ merger seems to have been effected in Southern Italy (as in Rome, cf. *infra*) during the course of the first half of the fourth century, and in Central Italy by the end of the fourth century; and (2) in Northern Italy during the course of the fourth/fifth-centuries. Actually, we do not have any specifically dated inscriptions from Northern Italy earlier than this time, which makes exact comparison with the rest of Italy difficult. Since Northern Italy and Lugdunensis seem to go hand in hand in matters of linguistic development,[42] it is not surprising that the inscriptions show that an intervocalic /b/ - /u̯/ merger seems to have taken place in both areas at approximately the same time.

Data concerning the use of *B* to represent interior /u̯/ in the inscriptions from Italy seem to give evidence of a geographical spread of the intervocalic /b/ - /u̯/ merger. As we move northward, the frequency of *B* as a misspelling for /u̯/ decreases from 50.3 % over-all in Southern Italy to 18.3 % and 18.7 % in Central and Northern Italy respectively. These figures would seem to lend support to the observations of Parodi (*op. cit.*, p. 191) and of Terracini (pp. 234-235), namely, that Southern Italy (together with

---

[40] Cited in G. Rohlfs, *Historische Grammatik der italienischen Sprache und ihres Mundarten* (Bern: A. Francke, 1949-154), Vol. 2, Sec. 167.

[41] C. H. Grandgent, *Introduction to Vulgar Latin* (1907; reprint New York: Hafner, 1962), Sec. 318.

[42] See P. Gaeng (pp. 150, 153, 156) where he notes a similarity in the evolution of Latin unstressed /ĕ/ and /ĭ/ in Lugdunensis and Northern Italy.

Rome) was a point of origin of the intervocalic /b/ - /u̯/ merger, which later spread northward in Italy and to other areas of the Empire.[43] We may also consider the possibility that the phenomenon in question may not have spread from one place to others, but may have begun spontaneously at different times in various places. The original consonantal system was about the same in all areas, and, all other things being equal, could be expected to evolve in the same way in all areas.

5.3 Conclusions

We may summarize our findings concerning the intervocalic /b/ - /u̯/ merger in North, Central, and Southern Italy as follows:

(1) The intervocalic /b/ - /u̯/ merger of Vulgar Latin took place in all three areas.

(2) Data concerning the existence of a Latin intervocalic /b/ - /u̯/ merger in Northern Italy in fourth/fifth-century inscriptions only show a predominance of V spellings for the expected intervocalic B spelling. It was found that more than half (nine out of fifteen) the examples of V for intervocalic B are found on inscriptions from the same place (the *Concordia* military cemetery) and may represent a localism only. There is no evidence to support the possibility that there may be a connection between a possible early voicing of Latin intervocalic /-p-/ > /-b-/ and the less frequent use of B for original /u̯/ in the North Italian inscriptions during this period. Data from Central and Southern Italian inscriptions show no preference for the use of V for intervocalic B.

(3) Data concerning an inconsistency in the use of the B and V spellings in the inscriptions from Southern Italy indicate a complete merger of the Latin /b/ and /u̯/.

---

[43] In an article entitled "A Research Report on Vulgar Latin and Its Local Variations," *Kratylos,* 9 (1964), 113-134, A. Tovar argues in favor of the possibility of the origin of the phenomenon in question in these areas and its spreading to others. He writes (pp. 129-130) thus: "Let us imagine ... that instead of a local Latin of Africa, or Spain or Gaul, we have specific centers of waves with diffuse phenomena: thus we can admit a center of *b/v* confusion first in Rome and Southern Italy."

136   THE EVOLUTION OF THE LATIN /b/ - /u̯/ MERGER

(4) According to the inscriptions, the development of an intervocalic /b/ - /u̯/ merger seems to have been effected in Southern Italy by the end of the fourth/early fifth centuries, about the same time it seems to have taken place in Central Italy. The phenomenon in question seems to have taken place in Northern Italy during the course of the fourth/fifth centuries. We cannot say how much earlier than this an intervocalic merger may have taken place in this area, since we do not have any dated inscriptions earlier than the fourth century.

(5) A merger in the intervocalic position of the originally distinct Latin /b/ and /u̯/ was a regular consonantal feature of the Vulgar Latin of Italy approximately four centuries prior to the appearance of Politzer and Goff's eighth-century documents from Northern and Central Italy respectively. (No systematic, quantitative analysis of documents from Southern Italy is available for a comparison with our inscriptions.)

(6) The inscriptions seem to give evidence of a spread of the intervocalic /b/ - /u̯/ merger northward from Southern Italy. This may, however, have simply begun spontaneously at approximately the same (or different) times in the various areas.

14. ROME

1. *Intervocalic Position*

1.1 CLat. *B* /b/

Area	Century	(B) → B	(B) → V	%
Rome	III/IV	56	4	6.7
	V	12	1	(7.7)
	VI/VII	6	2	25.0
	n. d.	162	5	3.0
	Totals	236	12	5.0

A number of examples of the use of *V* for intervocalic *B* appear in our inscriptional material from Rome. Following are examples from dated inscriptions, from third/fourth-century; inscriptional material (all examples are from the fourth century):

THE B-V ALTERNATION IN LATIN INSCRIPTIONS 137

INCOMPARAVILES (= INCOMPARABILIS) (*D.* 2732 a. 368)
EUSEVIO (*D.* 2807AN a. 359)
MIRAVILI (= MIRABILIS) (*D.* 4330 a. 308/312)
REVECCAE (= REBECCAE) (*D.* 4988 a. 397)

The only example from the fifth century is found in the adjective

AMAVILES (= AMABILIS) (*D.* 3112A a 485)

from sixth/seventh-century inscriptions:

SIVI (= SIBI) (*D.* 694 a. 522)
STAVILES (= STABILIS) (*D.* 2500 B VI cent.)

All deviations in undated inscriptions are found in indirect object pronominal forms:

SIVI (= SIBI) (*D.* 1545; *D.* 2711A; *D.* 3514)
TIVI (= TIBI) (*D.* 2258N); in the phrase PAX NOVISCUM (= NOBISCUM) (*D.* 2474)

The absence of a consistent pattern of deviations in dated inscriptions (the 6.7 % figure in third/fourth-century inscriptions is reduced to 3.4 %, since two out of the four deviations are found in proper nouns, the 7.7 % figure of fifth-century inscriptions is based on only one deviation and may represent the orthography of a single stonemason, the 25 % figure in sixth/seventh-century inscriptions is based on a total of only six occurrences of the expected interior *B* and two deviations with *V*), and a 3.0 % figure in undated inscriptions make it difficult to determine the stability of the Latin intervocalic /b/. Be that as it may, even if we leave the two deviations in proper nouns out of our count, we get a 4.1 % over-all figure, which would seem to point in the direction of a development that eventually resulted in an identification of /b/ with /u̯/ in the intervocalic position.

It was not necessary to give a tabular representation of data concerning the *B* /b/ in verb endings, since there are only three occurrences of the expected *B* here. The single cases of the expected *B* in dated inscriptions occurs in the form IMITABUNT (*D.* 4698), from the fourth century, and the remaining two occur on one and the same undated inscription which reads CANTABO BIRTUTEM TUAM ET EX[ULTA]BO MISERICORDIAM TUAM (D. 2414). These occurrences of the /b/ are included in our total figures, but not in those on the /b/ in intervocalic position (a procedure observed throughout this work).

1.2 CLat. V /u̯/

Century	(V) → V	(V) → B	%
III/IV	31	20	39.3
V	2	7	77.7
VI/VII	5	7	58.3
n. d.	159	110	41.2
Totals	197	144	41.5

A total of 144 examples of B spellings for the expected V in the intervocalic position are found in the inscriptions from Rome. Following are a few examples from dated inscriptions:

NOBE (= NOVEM) (D. 2904A a. 350)
VIBAS (= VIVAS) (D. 3315 a. 268)
BIBI (= VIVI) (D. 4146FN a. 400)
MAMBURTII (= the name of the consul MAVORTIUS a. 527) (D. 3157 a. 527)

from undated inscriptions:

NATIBITAS (= NATIVITAS) (D. 1537)
OTTABU (= OCTAVUS) (D. 4036)

We did not observe a consistent pattern of deviations from the spelling of the expected Latin intervocalic B /b/ in the inscriptions from Rome. On the other hand, the deviations from the spelling of the expected intervocalic V in third/fourth-century inscriptions (39.3 %) and the considerable increase in percentage figures in fifth and sixth/seventh-century inscriptions over the previous period (77.7 % and 58.3 % respectively), coupled with a 41.2 % figure in undated inscriptions, leave little doubt that a Latin intervocalic /b/ - /u̯/ merger was an accomplished fact in Rome by the time of the appearance of our Christian inscriptions from this area. If we leave 21 examples of B for intervocalic V

THE B-V ALTERNATION IN LATIN INSCRIPTIONS 139

in proper nouns out of our total count, we get a 38.4 % figure over-all. This latter figure, too, is conclusive as to an intervocalic /b/ - /u̯/ merger.

2. *Postconsonantal Position*

2.1 CLat. B /b/ after /l/

Century	(-LB-) → -LB-	(-LB-) → -LV-
III/IV	4	1
V	3	0
VI/VII	0	0
n. d.	0	0
Totals	7	1

There are seven occurrences of words with the expected -LB- spelling. The only example of the use of -LV- for -LB- is found on an inscription which reads in part, IN BASILICA ALVA (= ALBA, apparently with the meaning "new") (D. 3821 a. 391).

2.2 CLat. B /b/ after /r/

Century	(-RB-) → -RB-	(-RB-) → -RV-
III/IV	4	1
V	1	0
VI/VII	2	0
n. d.	11	0
Totals	18	1

There are a total of eighteen occurrences of words with -RB-. The only example of -RV- for -RB- is found in the form SUPER-VIA (D. 3546) from third/fourth-century inscriptions.

2.3 CLat. B after /s/

There are only three occurrences of words with the expected -SB-, all in undated inscriptions; hence the absence of a tabular representation. There is one example of the use of -SV- for -SB-. This occurs in a sixth-century inscription in the form PRESVI-TERO (D. 694 a. 522). We found a total of twenty-eight cases of the expected B in postconsonantal position and three deviations

140   THE EVOLUTION OF THE LATIN /b/ - /u̯/ MERGER

with *V* amounting to 9.7 %. This figure, since it is larger than five percent, cannot be dismissed. Let us also investigate the *V* spelling in postconsonantal position also.

2.4 CLat. *V* after /l/

Century	(-LV-) → -LV-	(-LV-) → -LB-	%
III/IV	0	0	
V	2	0	
VI/VII	0	0	
n. d.	2	4	66.6
Totals	4	4	50.0

There are four occurrences of words with the expected -*LV*-, and four deviations (all in undated inscriptions) with -*LB*-. With the exception of the form SALBO (= SALVO) (*D*. 1780), examples of the use of -*LB*- for -*LV*- are limited to proper nouns. They are:

SILBESTRO (*D*. 2591)
SILBINIANO (*D*. 3047)
SILBINE (*D*. 3818A)

The 50.0 % figure may be misleading, since three out of four deviations occur in proper nouns. These three may be of doubtful significance because of a possible lack of orthographic tradition.

2.5 CLat. *V* after /r/

Century	(-RV-) → -RV-	(-RV-) → -RB-	%
III/IV	2	1	
V	0	0	
VI/VII	2	1	
n. d.	1	6	
Totals	5	8	61.5

There are eight examples of the use of -*RB*- for -*RV*- in the inscriptions from Rome. As can be seen from the tables, deviations outnumber the correct forms. In dated inscriptions deviations occur in the following forms:

SERBABIT (= SERVAVIT) (*D*. 3429 a. 392)
PAREBULUS (= PARVULUS) (*D*. 4419 a. 522)

THE B-V ALTERNATION IN LATIN INSCRIPTIONS

In undated inscriptions we read:

SERBU (= SERVUS) (D. 1144aN)
OBSERBANS (= OBSERVANS) (D. 1339)
PARBUS (= PARVUS) (D. 1562)
PARBULA (= PARVULA) (D. 3548)
SERBULUS (= SERVULUS) (D. 4146C)

2.6 CLat. V after /d/

A tabular representation of this phenomenon was not necessary, since there are no occurrences of words with the expected -DV- (/du̯/). Examples (three) of the use of -DB- are found in undated inscriptions only. These are limited to the proper noun QUODVULTDEUS, which appears variously spelled as:

QUOBULDEO (D. 3137A)
COBBULDEUS (D. 3256B)
COBULDEUS (D. 4148N)

We found a total of nine cases of the expected V spelling in postconsonantal position and fifteen deviations (or 62.2 %) with B. If we leave a total of six deviations in proper nouns out of our count, our figure is reduced to 50.0 %. This figure, taken together with the 9.7 % figure showing the use of V for postconsonantal B indicates that a postconsonantal /b/ - /u̯/ merger took place in Rome, as it took place in Africa, and Southern Italy.

3. CLat. V /u̯/ in the perfect tense of REQUIE-VIT → REQUIE-BIT, and of other verbs

In this section data concerning the Latin V are restricted to the third person singular perfect tense ending of REQUIESCERE and of other verbs.

Century	(-VIT) → -VIT	(-VIT) → -BIT	%
III/IV	5	3	37.7
V	4	2	33.3
VI/VII	2	0	0.0
n. d.	13	15	53.5
Totals	24	20	45.4

Deviations occur in the following forms, from third/fourth-century inscriptions (deviations here are limited to the fourth cent.):

> PAUSABIT (D. 3239 a. 353)
> SERBABIT (= SERVAVIT) (D. 3429 a. 392)
> COMPARABIT (D. 3731 a. 363)

from the fifth century:

> COMPARABIT (= COMPARAVIT) (D. 3782 a. 465)
> COMPARABI (= COMPARAVIT) (D. 3789 B a. 403)

From undated inscriptions, several examples follow:

> AMABIT (D. 96b)
> EXIBIT, ESSIBE (= EXIVIT) (D. 2130; D. 2773A)
> REQUIEBIT (D. 3137; D. 3335)
> DONABIT (D. 3236)
> EDIFICABIT (= AEDIFICAVIT) (D. 3647)
> PERSERABIT (D. 4347)

3.1 *CLat.* V /u̯/ *in Other Perfect Tense Endings and in Other Verb Endings*

Data concerning Latin V /u̯/ in these endings are given in the following table. It will be seen that occurrences of the /u̯/ in these endings are infrequent and, in the perfect tense, deviations are limited to the first and third persons plural. In other verb endings, deviations occur in the second and third persons singular, future perfect active indicative/perfect active subjunctive (both endings are represented in Classical Latin by the forms -*VERIS* and -*VERIT*), and in the third person singular pluperfect active indicative. On the following page, we give the ratio of correct occurrences and deviations:

3.1a CLat. (V) /u/ in other perfect tense endings and other verb endings

A. first person singular perfect active indicative
B. first person plural perfect active indicative
C. third person plural perfect active indicative
D. other verb endings

Century	A (-VI) → -BI	(-VIMUS) → -BIMUS	B (-BERUNT)	C (-VERUNT) →	D OTHERS (V) → B	Tot. Cor.	Tot. Dev.	%
III/IV	0	0	0	1	0	1	0	
V	0	0	0	3	0	3	0	
VI/VII	0	0	0	0	0	0	0	
n. d.	2	0	1	2	3	4	10	71.4
Totals	2	0	1	6	3	8	10	55.5

3.1b *CLat.* V /u̯/ *in Other Perfect Tense Endings and in Other Verb Endings*

(a) *First Person Singular Perfect Active Indicative.*

There are two occurrences of the expected V in this verb ending and no deviations.

(b) *First Person Plural Perfect Active Indicative.*

There are no occurrences of this verb ending with the V, but there is one deviation in an undated inscription in the form CONPARABIM[US] (= COMPARAVIMUS) (*D.* 3727 H).

(c) *Third Person Plural Perfect Active Indicative.*

There are a total of six instances of the expected V spelling in this ending, and six deviations with B. All deviations are found in undated inscriptions and are limited to the verb form COMPARABERUNT[T] (*D.* 3727HN; *D.* 3733; *D.* 3736; *D.* 3755; *D.* 3772; and *D.* 3818).

(d) *Other Verb Endings.*

There are no occurrences of the expected V spelling in other verb endings. However, there are three examples of the use of B for V, all in undated inscriptions. In the second and third persons singular, future perfect active indicative/perfect active subjunctive endings we found:

HORABERIS (= ORAVERIS) (*D.* 3837)
BIOLABERIT (= VIOLAVERIT) (*D.* 3844)

In the third person singular perfect active indicative we found the form PREPARABERAT for PRAEPARAVERAT (*D.* 3866).

3.2 SUMMARY: *The Latin* V /u̯/ *in All Perfect Tense Endings and in Other Verb Endings Together*

We shall now summarize our data concerning the Latin V in these verb endings as evidence of a possible Latin intervocalic /b/ - /u̯/ merger in Rome. Our method in this connection will consist in giving a table showing total occurrences of the expected V in these verb endings and detherefrom, together with percentage figures (a procedure we followed in connection with similar data

THE B-V ALTERNATION IN LATIN INSCRIPTIONS 145

from the other Italian areas (*supra*, Italy, Sec. 3.4). The ratio of correct occurrences and deviations is as follows:

Area	Century	(V) → B		%
	III/IV	6	3	33.3
	V	7	2	22.2
	VI/VII	2	0	0.0
	n. d.	17	25	59.5
	Totals	32	30	48.4

The 33.3 % figure in third/fourth-century inscriptions and the 22.2 % figure in fifth-century inscriptions are based on a total of only nine possible occurrences of the /u̯/ in verb endings. The decrease in the percentage of deviations in sixth/seventh-century inscriptions to 0.0 % may be due to the fact that there are only a total of two occurrences of the /u̯/ in verb endings during this period. However, the number of instances of *B* for *V* (which outnumber the correct forms) in undated inscriptions, and the overall 48.4 % figure based on thirty-two occurrences of the expected *V* spelling and thirty deviations with *B* leaves little doubt that Rome shows a pattern of deviations from the expected *V* spelling in verb endings very similar to that observed in Southern Italy and Africa. The conclusion that the over-all 48.4 % figure represents an intervocalic /b/ - /u̯/ marger in this area is logical.

4. *Initial Position*

4.1 CLat. *B* /b/

Area	Century	(B) → B	(B) → V	%
Rome	III/IV	57	1	1.7
	V	7	0	0.0
	VI/VII	18	2	10.0
	n. d.	228	19	7.8
	Totals	310	22	6.3

Deviations from the spelling of the expected initial *B* occur in the following forms, from third/fourth-century inscriptions:

VONE (= BONAE) (*D*. 2805 a. 387)

from sixth/seventh-century inscriptions:

>   VOETIO (= BOETIO) (*D.* 840 a. 522)
>   VISQUE (= BISQUE) (*D.* 1092 a. 546)

In undated inscriptions, sixteen out of nineteen deviations occur in the form VENE(MERENTI) for BENE(MERENTI) (*D.* 2591; *D.* 2594; *D.* 2874BN; *D.* 3098A, etc.). Other V spellings for initial B in undated inscriptions are found in the following forms:

>   VISOMUM (= BISOMUM) (*D.* 3813; *D.* 3814)
>   VISCANDENTE (= BISCANDENTE) (*D.* 3813AN)

4.2 CLat. V /u̯/

Area	Century	(V) → V	(V) → B	%
Rome	III/IV	156	27	15,3
	V	64	13	17.3
	VI/VII	28	5	8.3
	n. d.	432	280	38.7
	Totals	680	325	32.3

A total of 154 out of 325 examples of the use of B for initial V occur in the verb form VIXIT, which appears variously spelled as BIXXIT (*D.* 4572), BIXIT (*D.* 4011B), BIXSIT (*D.* 4580), BISIT (*D.* 3802), BISSIT (*D.* 2597), and BICXSIT (*D.* 4005A). Examples of deviations in other than this verb form are, from third/fourth-century inscriptions:

>   BIGINTI (= VIGINTI) (*D.* 2940A a. 350)
>   BAPET (= VADET) (*D.* 4379 a. 386)

from sixth/seventh-century inscriptions:

>   BIBA (= VIVA) (*D.* 3727G a. 542/565)
>   BIRO (= VIRO) (*D.* 841 a. 584)

from undated inscriptions:

>   BENERA (BILIS) (= VENERABILIS) (*D.* 1563)
>   BIDHUE (= VIDUA) (*D.* 1736)
>   BENITE (= VENITE) (*D.* 2477N)
>   BOLO (= VOLO) (*D.* 4432B)

5. Summary and Conclusions

Our inscriptional material from Rome offers sufficient evidence of an intervocalic /b/ - /u̯/ merger. In order to show the reader the trend of this merger, and to make our comparison with the rest of Italy complete, we give the following summary tables showing the treatment of the Latin /b/ and /u̯/ in the interior position. This will give over-all percentage figures. We will also examine the possible chronology of this merger. The ratio of total correct occurrences and deviations is as follows:

5a. *Comparative Tables Concerning the Treatment of the Latin /b/ and /u̯/ in the Interior Position in Rome*

Century	(B) → V		%	(V) → B		%
III/IV	65	6	8.5	39	24	32.9
V	16	1	(5.9)	11	9	45.0
VI/VII	8	3	27.2	9	8	47.1
n. d.	178	5	2.7	179	148	45.2
Totals	267	15	5.3	238	189	44.2

5.1 SUMMARY: *The Latin /b/ and /u̯/ in the Interior Position*

It would be difficult for us to make any general statement concerning the stability of the Latin /b/ on the basis of deviations from the spelling of the expected interior *B*, if it were not for the 8.5 % figure (sixty-five occurrences of the expected *B* and six deviations with *V*) in third/fourth-century inscriptions. The 5.9 % figure in fifth-century inscriptions based on only a single deviation may represent the orthography of a single stonemason. The 27.2 % figure in sixth/seventh-century inscriptions is based on only eight occurrences of the expected interior *B* and three deviations with *V*. The low 2.7 % figure in undated inscriptions does not lend much support to those obtained in the inscriptions from these latter two periods. Be that as it may, the over-all number of instances in which the *V* is used for the expected interior *B* (fifteen examples of *V* to 267 cases of the expected *B*, or 5.3 %) probably indicates a weakening of the Latin consonant symbolized by *B* and its merger with that normally written a *V*. If we leave two deviations in proper nouns out of our count, we get a 4.8 %

figure. Although this is a borderline figure, it would seem to point in the direction of a development that eventually resulted in a merger of /b/ and /u̯/ in the interior position.

On the other hand, the figures presented in our table show that in each of the periods examined, and in undated inscriptions, the interior /u̯/ is represented by *B* with a significantly higher frequency than is the case of /b/ represented by *V*. The consistently increasing pattern of percentage of deviation from the expected spelling of the interior /u̯/ in dated inscriptions (32.9 % in third/fourth-century inscriptions, to 45.0 % in the fifth century, to 47.1 % in sixth/seventh-century inscriptions), coupled with the 45.2 % figure in undated inscriptions, and the 44.2 % figure over-all leave little doubt that a /b/ - /u̯/ merger in interior position was an accomplished fact in Rome by the time of the appearance of our Christian inscriptions from this area. If we leave a total of twenty-seven deviations in proper nouns out of our count, the over-all 44.2 % is reduced to 40.5 %. This figure is equally conclusive that the Latin /b/ and /u̯/ had merged in this position.

5.2 SUMMARY: *The Latin /b/ and /u̯/ in the Initial Position*

Data concerning the use of *V* for initial *B* parallel those concerning the use of *V* for interior *B*, namely an absence of a consistent pattern of deviations. The 1.7 % figure in third-fourth-century inscriptions is based on a single deviation as against fifth-seven cases of the expected initial *B*. This may represent the orthography of a single stonemason. The decrease in the percentage of deviation in fifth-century inscriptions to 0.0 % may be due to the fact that there are only a total of seven occurrences of the initial /b/ in this century, i.e., one-eighth the occurrences with respect to the previous centuries, and approximately one-third the occurrences with respect to the later centuries. The 10.0 % figure in sixth/seventh-century inscriptions may be misleading, since it is based on only two deviations (one in a proper noun) as against eighteen cases of the expected initial *B*. However, the nineteen deviations with *V* (7.8 %) in undated inscriptions and the twenty-two deviations with *V* over-all (6.3 %) cannot be dismissed.

Data concerning the use of *B* for initial *V* correlate well with those found in the interior position, namely a predominance of *B* spellings for *V* beginning with inscriptions from the third/fourth centuries and continuing into the later centuries, and in undated inscriptions as well. If we leave a total of forty-four deviations in proper nouns out of our total count, we get a 29.2 % figure. Thus, we find a *B-V* alternation in initial position going both ways: *B* words with *V* spellings, and *V* words with *B* spellings, and the frequency of such misspellings is not negligible in either direction. From this we conclude the existence of a Latin /b/ - /u̯/ merger in initial position in Rome.

In connection with a possible chronology of a Latin /b/ - /u̯/ merger in Rome, we note that the earliest dated inscription in our corpus which shows a *B-V* alternation occurs in the form VIBAS (= VIVAS) (*D.* 3315) and is dated 268 A. D. Are we to interpret this single instance of an intervocalic *B-V* confusion in the light of Grandgent's statement regarding the chronology of the intervocalic /b/ - /u̯/ merger in Italy, namely that "it was completed in Italy by the third [century]" (Sec. 318)? On the basis of a single deviation, any general statement in this regard is highly questionable and hypothetical. Grandgent's generalization seems to need modification to the effect that, at least on the basis of some specifically dated inscriptions, a Latin /b/ - /u̯/ merger (intervocalic and initial) seems to have been effected in Rome during the course of the first half of the fourth century. (There is no separate section designated *Conclusions,* since the data for this area are quite straightforward.)

Part III

SUMMARY OF FINDINGS AND CONCLUSIONS

It would be well to summarize our data concerning the use of *B* and *V* in our corpus of inscriptions from the Empire, and to bring under one heading the conclusions reached in the body of the work. On the following pages, we give in tabular form our total figures showing the *B-V* alternation in the various areas under study.

SUMMARY OF FINDINGS AND CONCLUSIONS 151

Comparative Summary Table Concerning the Latin (B) → V

A. Intervocalic Position
B. Postconsonantal Position
C. Verb Endings
D. Initial Position

Area	A (B)→V	%	B (B)→V	%	C (B)→V	%	D (B)→V	%	Tot. Cor. (B)→V	Tot. Dev.	%
Britain (Pagan)	95	1 (10.4)	7	0	0.0	0	0	71	0	0.0	173	1	(0.6)
Britain (Christ.)	11	0	0.0	0		0	0	9	0	0.0	20	0	0.0
Balkans (Pagan)	28	2	6.6	0	0.0	0	0	19	0	0.0	47	2	4.1
Balkans (Christ.)	20	0	0.0	5	0.0	1	0.0	22	1	(4.3)	48	1	(2.0)
Dalmatia	71	2	2.7	3	1 (25.0)	2	1 (33.3)	38	2	5.0	114	6	5.0
No. Africa	114	4	3.3	18	4 18.3	10	3 23.0	131	4	2.9	273	15	5.2

The Latin (B) → V (Continued)

Area	A (B)→V		%	B (B)→V		%	C (B)→V		%	D (B)→V		%	Tot. Cor. (B)→V	Tot. Dev.	%
Spain															
Baetica	22	1	(4.3)	3		0.0	0			33	0	0.0	58	1	(1.7)
Lusitania	11	1	(8.3)	1		0.0	0			7	0	0.0	19	1	(5.0)
Tarraconen.	21	0	0.0	4	1	(20.0)	0			14	1	6.6	39	2	4.9
Gaul															
Lugdunensis	79	20	20.2	2	2	50.0	0			98	0	0.0	179	22	10.9
Narbonensis	74	5	6.3	8	0	0.0	0			117	0	0.0	199	5	2.5
Italy															
Northern	85	8	8.6	8	0	0.0	19	10	34.4	101	0	0.0	213	18	7.8
Central	77	8	8.3	3	0	0.0	0			83	3	3.4	163	8	4.7
Southern	83	3	3.5	5	2	28.5	0			127	4	3.1	215	9	4.0
Rome	236	12	5.0	28	3	9.7	3	0	0.0	310	22	6.3	577	37	6.0

SUMMARY OF FINDINGS AND CONCLUSIONS

Comparative Summary Table Concerning the Latin (V) → B

A. Intervocalic Position
B. Postconsonantal Position
C. Verb Endings
D. Initial Position

Area	A (V)→B	%	B (V)→B	%	C (V)→B	%	D (V)→B	%	Tot. Cor. (V)→B	Tot. Dev.	%
Britain (Pagan)	119	0.0	38	0.0	25	0.0	338	0.6	520	2	0.4
Britain (Christ.)	20	0.0	2	0.0	6	25.0	16	0.0	44	2	4.3
Balkans (Pagan)	31	0.0	5	0.0	1	0.0	113	0.0	150	0	0.0
Balkans (Christ.)	20	0.0	1	0.0	4	(25.0)	70	0.0	95	1	(10.5)
Dalmatia	59	10.6	14	12.5	18	21.7	169	4.7	260	22	7.7
No. Africa	119	23.7	48	31.4	46	48.3	532	12.5	745	177	19.1

The Latin (V) → B (Continued)

Area	A (V)→B		%	B (V)→B		%	C (V)→B		%	D (V)→B		%	Tot. Cor. (V)→B	Tot. Dev.	%
Spain															
Baetica	17	5	22.7	8	0	0.0	7	0	0.0	108	0	0.0	140	5	3.4
Lusitania	14	2	12.5	0	1	(100.0)	54	4	7.0	91	0	0.0	159	7	2.6
Tarraconen.	25	4	13.7	0	1	(100.0)	10	5	33.3	79	2	2.4	114	12	9.5
Gaul															
Lugdunensis	46	2	4.2	6	0	0.0	13	5	27.7	266	2	0.8	331	9	2.6
Narbonensis	30	3	9.1	5	0	0.0	15	3	16.6	212	4	1.9	262	10	3.6
Italy															
Northern	82	18	18.0	14	6	30.0	38	7	15.6	490	20	3.9	624	51	7.5
Central	56	16	22.2	19	3	13.6	23	3	11.5	258	11	4.0	356	33	8.4
Southern	47	45	48.9	14	7	33.3	17	27	61.4	228	96	29.6	406	175	30.1
Rome	197	144	41.5	9	15	62.5	32	30	48.4	680	325	32.3	918	514	35.8

SUMMARY OF FINDINGS AND CONCLUSIONS   155

I. *The Geographical Extension of the Phenomenon*

Our tables show that a *B-V* alternation took place in varying degrees of frequency in the Latin inscriptions found in the Roman provinces of Dalmatia, North Africa, Spain, Gaul, and Italy. It did not occur to any great extent in Britain and the Balkans.

II. *Intervocalic Position*

1. Data from the inscriptions concerning the use of *B* and *V* show a paucity of evidence of a possible identification of Latin intervocalic /b/ and /u̯/ in Britain and the Balkans. Evidence of stability of the Latin /b/ and /u̯/ means an absence of merger of the two in intervocalic position in these areas. The late preservation of the phonemic distinction between intervocalic /b/ and /u̯/ constitutes a regional isogloss for these two areas.

1.1 Evidence from the inscriptions showing an inconsistency in the use of the letters *B* and *V* shows the existence of an intervocalic /b/ - /u̯/ merger in all areas of the Western Roman Empire where Romance speech later developed, viz. Spain, Gaul, Italy, and Dalmatia, as well as in North Africa, where Latin did not survive in the form of a Romance language. In this respect, the evolution of the Latin intervocalic /b/ and /u̯/ in North Africa parallels the evolution of these two consonants in all areas of the Empire (except Britain and the Balkans), and distinguishes itself as the least conservative peripheral Latin-speaking area.

1.2 Evidence from inscriptions of a Latin intervocalic /b/ - /u̯/ merger shows a broad geographical extension comprising both the so-called "East" and "West" Romance dialect areas. Clearly, then, in Dalmatia no regional partitioning can be drawn for this feature of the consonantal system, as the intervocalic /b/ - /u̯/ merger took place in such geographically contiguous areas as Central and Northern Italy, i.e. "East" and "West" Romance dialect areas, as well as in areas as far removed geographically as Gaul and North Africa.

1.3 Our tables show a remarkable discrepancy in the use of *B* for original /u̯/, in contrast with a lower frequency of *V* for original /b/. We give our figures concerning the *B* and *V* spellings in intervocalic position in the various areas where a merger took place. Consistent instances of this found in Dalmatia (1.4 % V for /b/: 9.2 % B for /u̯/), North Africa (3.5 % V for /b/: 23.2 % B for /u̯/), Spain (3.6 % V for /b/: 13.4 % B for /u̯/), Gaul (Narbonensis only) (6.3 % V for /b/: 9.1 % B for /u̯/), Italy (No., Ce., St.) (7.1 % V for /b/: 29.9 % B for /u̯/), and Rome (5.0 % V for /b/: 41.5 % B for /u̯/) might suggest that this skewing is due to more than just a chance distribution. To explain this distribution as a result of a widespread orthographic practice on the part of stonemasons from these areas might lead one to question on what basis we decide that we are confronted by orthography vs. phonology. On the other hand, can this skewing in favor of the use of B for original /u̯/ reflect what P. Gaeng (p. 100 note 64) calls a "spirantization of the labiovelar phoneme," i.e. a strengthening of the articulation of the original semiconsonant /u̯/, probably as a bilabial fricative [β]? If so, this would be in agreement with the beliefs of Romance philologists who have always agreed that there was probably a bilabial stage at first everywhere in proto-Romance, because in the articulation of a labiovelar semiconsonant /u̯/ there is a slight protrusion of both lips. Perhaps also, in the B regions the bilabial stage lasted longer. This is hypothetical, but possible.

On the other hand, Lugdunensis is the only area where an intervocalic merger took place which shows a skewing in favor of V spellings for original /b/ (20.2 % V for /b/: 4.2 % B for /u̯/). Is the contrast between these data from Lugdunensis and those from other regions to be explained as due to regional differences? If so, Lugdunensis would be most innovating in this respect. We have also considered the possibility that there may be a connection between a possible early voicing of Latin intervocalic /-p-/ > /-b-/ and the low frequency of B for original /u̯/ in this region. A similar phenomenon occurs in the fourth/fifth-century inscriptions from Northern Italy. But here it was observed that nine out of fifteen examples of the use of V for original /b/ were found in the same place (*Concordia* military cemetery) and may represent a localism only. There was no evidence from the North Italian inscriptions of a relationship between a possible early voicing of Latin intervocalic /-p-/ to /-b-/ and the low frequency of B for original /u̯/ in this area in the early centuries.

II. Postconsonantal Position

1. Deviations from the expected postconsonantal *B* and *V* spellings amounting to more than 5 % in North Africa (18.3 % *V* for /b/: 31.4 % *B* for /u̯/), Southern Italy (28.7 % *V* for /b/: 33.3 % *B* for /u̯/), and Rome (9.7 % *V* for /b/: 62.5 % *B* for /u̯/) seem to suggest that this spelling alternation has its source in a postconsonantal /b/ - /u̯/ merger.

1.1 In Northern and Central Italy there are no deviations from the expected postconsonantal *B* spellings. In these areas, *B* spellings for *V* amounting to more than 5 % (30 % in Northern Italy and 13.6 % in Central Italy) may be a reflection of a strengthening of the postconsonantal /u̯/. Deviations in other areas are negligible or non-existant.

III. Verb Endings

1. Data concerning Latin /b/ *(B)* in verb endings show that deviations occur only in Dalmatia (only one), North Africa, and Northern Italy. Three deviations are found in North Africa (one each in the first, second, and third persons, singular, future active indicative). The highest percentage figure showing *V* spelling for Latin /b/ in verb endings occurs in Northern Italy. Here deviations (9) are limited to the spelling of the verb form DABIT, which appears in stereotyped formulae, all found in the *Concordia* military cemetery.

1.1 Examples of *B* spellings for Latin /u̯/ in verb endings, which are especially represented by the verb form REQUIEVIT, are found in inscriptions from all areas, except those from pagan Britain and the Balkans, and Christian inscriptions from Baetica. This phenomenon is particularly frequent in the inscriptions from North Africa, Southern Italy, and Rome, which show percentage figures as high as 46.1 %, 61.4 %, and 48.4 % respectively. In Spain, the Tarraconensis area shows the highest percentage of *B* spellings for Latin /u̯/ in verb endings, and sets itself apart from other Spanish areas as far as frequency of deviations goes.

IV. Initial Position

1. Based on reliable percentage figures, deviations amounting to less than five percent are found in Britain, the Balkans, Dalmatia, Spain, Gaul, and Northern and Central Italy. We conclude that the Latin /b/ and /u̯/ remained distinct in initial position in these areas.

1.1 Inconsistency in the use of the expected initial *B* and *V* spellings in the Latin inscriptions from North Africa, Southern Italy, and Rome suggests a Latin /b/ - /u̯/ merger in this position in these areas.

PART IV

THE EVOLUTION OF
THE LATIN /b/ AND /u̯/: OTHER SOURCES

We now know what a quantitative-comparative analysis of the *B* and *V* spellings based on internal evidence from the Latin inscriptions themselves has revealed concerning the phonemic status of the Latin /b/ and /u̯/ in the various areas of the Empire. What remains is to compare these findings with information about Vulgar Latin drawn from elsewhere, i.e., scholars who have given some consideration to the phenomenon in question, and the development of these two classical Latin sounds in the Romance dialects.

1. *The Antiquity of the Phenomenon*

Data from the inscriptions show the continuation of a process whose beginnings have been traced back to the first century of our era. Authorities on Latin phonetics agree that the *B* represented a voiced bilabial occlusive /b/ before the first century of our era and that it later weakened (lost its occlusive articulation) as [β], and merged with the /u̯/ *(V)*, a voiced labiovelar semi-consonant, which is said to have also developed a bilabial fricative aritculation [β] in the first century of our era.[1] The oldest ortho-

---

[1] R. G. Kent, *The Sounds of Latin* (Baltimore: Waverly Press, 1943), Secs. 44, 48, 49, 61, 78; W. M. Lindsay, *The Latin Language* (Oxford: Clarendon Press, 1894), Secs. 48, 49, 78; E. H. Sturtevant *The Pronunciation of Greek and Latin*, 2nd ed. (Philadelphia: Linguistic Society of America, 1940), pp. 142-143, 174; L. Palmer, *The Latin Language* (London:

graphic evidence of a /b/ - /u̯/ confusion is found in that century. Citing his sources, C. H. Grandgent (*op. cit.*, Sec. 316) gives examples showing an inconsistency in the use of B and V in the inscriptions from the second century, e.g., BIVERE, BALVIS, VIBIT. The testimony of Latin grammarians of the third century concerning the almost universal confusion in the use of the B and V is taken as evidence that a merger of original Latin intervocalic /b/ and /u̯/ was well underway, if not completed, by this time. Already in the "Appendix Probi," the grammarian Probus cautions thus: #9 BACULUS NON VACLUS, #44 BRAVIUM NON BRABIUM, #70 ALVEUS NON ALBEUS, #91 PLEBES NON PLEVIS, #93 TABES NON TAVIS, #198 TOLERABILIS NON TOLERAVILIS, #215 VAPULO NON BAPLO.[2]

2. *Latin Sources of the Romance /b, ƀ, and v/*

In order to provide a framework to compare our findings concerning the /b/ and /u̯/ in the inscriptions with the evolution of these two consonants in the Romance languages, we devote space in the following two sections to data in existing Romance languages and dialects.[3]

Faber and Faber, 1954), Secs. 48-9; Max Niederman, *Précis de phonétique historique du latin*, 4th ed. (Paris: Klincksieck, 1953), pp. 87-88.

[2] Cited in W. D. Elcock, *The Romance Languages* (London: Faber and Faber, 1960), p. 31. There is some question whether Probus' cautions were against errors in spelling or against errors in pronunciations. Elcock (p. 29) gives a summary of the beliefs of various scholars concerning this matter. Elcock himself believes that Probus was concerned with errors in spelling. He writes *(ibid.)* "A close examination of the data suggests that his concern was not so much with pronunciation as with spelling. ... The many 'hypercorrect' forms ... seem to pertain to orthography rather than to pronunciation. ... We therefore incline towards the idea that the list was complied by a schoolmaster, much as a teacher of English today might draw up a list of common errors in spelling culled from the exercises of his pupils; but in a Roman class-room, just as they would nowadays, many such errors had their origin in current pronunciation." In our own material, we have found that in most areas a B-V alternation in intervocalic position has its source in phonological change, while in most areas (except North Africa, Southern Italy, and Rome), a B-V alternation in initial position is due to spelling mistakes of stonemasons.

[3] The main sources of the data presented in these paragraphs are the following: Heinrich Lausberg, *Lingüística romanica*, trans. J. Pérez Riesco and E. Pascual Rodríguez, Vol. I (Madrid: Editorial Gredos), Secs. 300-

The majority of Romance dialects have two distinct voiced labial consonants, the voiced bilabial occlusive /b/ and the voiced labiodental fricative /v/. The Romance /b/ came from the Latin initial and postconsonantal /b/: BENE, ALBA > Fr. *bien*, It. *bene*, Prov. *ben;* Fr. *aube*, It. *alba*, Prov. *alba*. In Western Romance, Latin intervocalic /-p-/ voiced to /b/ after the intervocalic /b/ - /u̯/ merger took place. In France, this /-b-/ < /-p-/ became /v/: RIPA > *rive*.

We postulate here a single voiced bilabial fricative /ƀ/,[4] which developed from Latin initial /u̯/ and Latin intervocalic /b/ and /u̯/ as the source of the modern Romance labiodental /v/, initial and intervocalic: VENIT > Fr. *vient*, It. *viene*, Prov. *ven;* DĒBĒRE > Fr. *devoir*, It. *devere*, Prov. *dever;* LAVARE > Fr. *laver*, It. *lavare*, Prov. *lavar*. (There are some words in Italian which retain the original Latin intervocalic /b/: DUBITAT, DEBITA > It. *dubita, debita*.)

A single voiced bilabial phoneme with strong and weak variants [b - ƀ] is found in Castilian and Gascon. This consonant represents a complete merger of the originally distinct Romance /b/ and /v/.

3. *The /b, ƀ, and v/ in Existing Romance Languages and Dialects*

We may now compare our findings concerning the status of the Latin /b/ and /u̯/ on the basis of inscriptions from those areas of the Roman World where Romance speech later developed with its distribution in existing Romance languages and dialects.[5]

A. *Intervocalic Position.* Evidence from the inscriptions from Gaul, Spain, and Italy shows the existence of a Latin intervocalic

---

301, 364, 373; M. A. Pei, *The Italian Language* (New York: S. F. Vanni and Co., 1949), Sec. 91; F. H. Jungemann, *La teoría del sustrato*, Chap. XV.

[4] Theodoro Henrique Maurer, Jr., *Gramática do Latim Vulgar* (Rio de Janeiro: Livraria Academica, 1959), p. 35, note 88, gives an account of the beliefs of various scholars concerning the nature of the sound resulting from the intervocalic /b/ - /u̯/ merger.

[5] Data on these dialects presented in the following paragraph are from M. K. Pope, *From Latin to Modern French*, Sec. 336; R. Menéndez-Pidal, *Manual de gramática histórica española*, Sec. 32a; M. A. Pei, *The Italian Language*, Secs. 90-91; W. Meyer-Lübke, *Grammatica storica della lingua italiana e dei dialetti toscani*, Secs. 98, 112; M. L. Wagner, *Historische Lautlehre des Sardischen*, Secs. 121-122, 150-159; H. Tiktin, *Romänisches Elementarbuch*, pp. 54-56.

THE EVOLUTION OF THE LATIN /b/ - /u̯/ MERGER

/b/ - /u̯/ merger. In all Romance languages, the Latin /b/ and /u̯/ have merged in the intervocalic position. There is no evidence from the Latin inscriptions from the Romanized inner Balkan region of the existence of an intervocalic /b/ - /u̯/ merger (or of the loss of Latin intervocalic /-b-/, which subsequently took place in Roumanian).

B. Initial Position. In this position, a /b/ - /u̯/ merger did not take place in all Romance languages and dialects. The distribution of the Romance /b, ƀ, and v/ in this position may be summarized briefly as follows:

1. In Standard French and Italian and in Old Spanish the Latin /u̯/ became /v/ (labiodental) and remained distinct from the /b/ in initial position: BONU > Fr. *bon*, It. *buono*, Sp. *bueno*; VILLA > Fr. *ville*, It. *villa*, Sp. *villa*. This corroborates well with data from the inscriptions from Gaul, Italy (North and Central), and Spain where we found evidence of stability of the Latin initial /b/ and /u̯/, indicating the conservation of the phonemic distinction in this position.

2. In Castilian and neighboring Hispano-Romance dialects and in Gascon and neighboring dialects of southwestern France, the two originally distinct Romance consonants /b/ and /v/ have merged in all positions as a single voiced bilabial phoneme with occlusive-fricative variants [b - ƀ].[6] In Spanish the letters *b* and *v* are used to represent this phoneme, but in most cases the orthography is etymological. In absolute initial position, after a word ending in a nasal consonant, and in internal position after a nasal, the occlusive, or strong, variant [b] occurs: BASIU > *beso*, [beso] UNU BASIU > *un beso* [umbeso], AMBOS > *ambos* [ambos]; VINU > *vino* [bino], UNU VINU > *un vino* [umbino], CUM VENIT > *conviene* [kombi̯ene]. In all other positions the fricative, or weak, variant [ƀ] occurs: ISTE BASIU > *este beso* [esteƀeso], ILLE BASIU > *el beso* [elƀeso], DABAT > *daba* [daƀa]; ISTE VINU > *este vino* [esteƀino], ILLE VINU > *el vino* [elƀino], LAVABAT > *lavaba* [laƀaƀa] (in Old Spanish *daba* and *lavaba*

---

[6] T. Navarro Tomás, *Manual de pronunciación española* (Secs. 90-91) gives detailed phonetic descriptions and an account of the allophonic distribution of the Spanish phoneme discussed here.

were spelled *dava* and *lavava*). There is no evidence in the Latin inscriptions from Spain or Gaul of a possible beginning of a complete merger of original Latin /b/ and /u̯/.

3. In existing Italo-Romance dialects in Sardinia, parts of Sicily, and Southern Italy a complete merger of the Latin /b/ and /u̯/ is general. In central and southern Sardinia, a /b/ - /u̯/ merger exists as occlusive [b] in strong positions, and fricative or weak [b̬] everywhere else, i. e. in essentially the same way as in Spanish and Gascon. Rohlfs (Sec. 167) points out that in most of Sicily and southern Italy the initial /b/ and /u̯/ are merged as /v/, not /b/, e. g. *bastone* /vastone/, *bocca* /voka/. He points out *(ibid.)* that in some southern Italian dialects, forms with /v/ may not represent words in absolute initial position. Here, after words with a strong articulation, initial /v/ becomes /b/; /b/ remains: nonstandard Sicilian /tri bbakki/ 'tre vacche', Calabrian /e bbestutu/ 'e vestito', Southern Apulian /nu bbisciu/ 'non vedo', Neapolitan /abbecino/ 'da vicino'; /tri bbasi/ 'tre baci'. It would not be unreasonable to interpret the *B - V* alternation in all positions in the inscriptions from Southern Italy as evidence of a possible beginning of this complete merger of the Latin /b/ and /u̯/ in the Vulgar Latin from this area.

4. In Roumanian, a Latin /b/ - /u̯/ merger exists in some cases in initial and postconsonantal positions: VETERANUS > *batrîn*, SERVIRE > *serbire*. There is no evidence in the inscriptions of a possible beginning of this phenomenon in the Vulgar Latin of the inner Balkans.

It is now clear that a quantitative-comparative analysis of data from inscriptions can show that in most areas of the Empire the original articulations of the Latin /b/ and /u̯/ were changing, while in others they were preserved. The implications are clear: By examining the internal evidence from the inscriptions themselves, by establishing a criterion to separate errors in spelling from errors which are interpreted as indications of phonological change, it has been possible to show that Latin was evolving throughout the Empire at times showing similar developments in some areas and at times showing differences in its evolution with regard to the phenomenon in question.

The treatment of the original Latin /b/ and /u̯/ was not uniform in all areas. In the lateral areas (Britain and the Balkans) these two consonants seemed not to have changed, in all other areas they merged in intervocalic position, and in some they merged in all positions. The sound change started at different times in the different dialects, and its chronology differed from area to area. These similarities and differences already existing in the Latin of the Empire can be traced into the Romance languages. Even if the Romance languages never developed (as one did not develop in North Africa), at least with respect to the phenomenon in question, inscriptions could be used as a reliable source for studying the evolution of Latin in the various areas of the Empire.

BIBLIOGRAPHY

Primary Sources

Corpus Inscriptionum Latinarum, consilio et auctoritate Academiae Litterarum Borussicae editum. Berlin, 1863-1943.
Collingwood, R. G., and Wright, R. P. *The Roman Inscriptions of Britain.* Vol. I. Oxford: Clarendon Press, 1965.
Altlateinische Inschriften. 4th ed. Ed. Ernst Diehl. Berlin: Walter de Gruyter, 1959.
Inscriptiones Latinae Christianae Veteres. 3 vols. Ed. Ernst Diehl. Berlin: Weidman, 1925-31. Vol. IV is the Supplement to *Inscriptiones Latinae Christianae Veteres,* edited by J. Moreau and H. I. Marrou. Berlin: Weidman, 1967.
Vulgärlateinische Inschriften. Ed. Ernst Diehl. Bonn: Marcus u. Weber, 1910.
Inscriptiones Britanniae Christianae. Ed. Emil Hübner. Berlin: Georg Reimer, 1876.
Antike Denkmäler in Bulgarien. Ed. Ernst Kalinka. Schriften der Balkankommissien. Vol. IV. Vienna: Alfred Hölder, 1906.
Macalister, R.A.S. *Corpus Inscriptionum Insularum Celticarum.* Vol. I. Dublin: Stationery Office, 1945.
Vives, José (ed.). *Inscripciones cristianas de la España Romana y Visigoda.* Barcelona: J. M. Viader, 1942.

Chief Works Used

Bartoli, Matteo G. *Das Dalmatische: Altromanische Sprachreste von Veglia bis Ragusa und ihre Stellung in der apennino-balkanischen Romania.* 2 vols. Schriften der Balkancommission, Nos. IV, V. Vienna: Alfred Hölder, 1906.
———. *Introduzione alla neolinguistica.* Biblioteca dell' "Archivum Romanicum," Serie II, *Linguistica,* Vol. 12. Geneva: Olschki, 1925.
Battisti, Carlo. *Avviamento Allo Studio del Latino Volgare.* Bari: Leonardo da Vinci Editrice, 1949.
Blaise, Albert. *Manuel du latin chrétien.* Strasbourg: Le Latin Chrétien, 1955.
———. *Précis historique de phonétique française.* 9th ed. Revised. Paris: Klincksieck, 1958.

Bloch, Raymond. *L'Epigraphie latine.* 4th ed. Paris: Presses Universitaires de France, 1969.

Bourciez, Édouard. *Éléments de linguistique romane.* 5th ed. Paris: Klincksieck, 1967.

Brüch, Josef. Review of "A Chronology of Vulgar Latin," by H. F. Muller. *Zeitschrift für französische Sprache und Literatur,* 54 (1931), 357-82.

Budinszky, Alexander. *Die Ausbreitung der lateinischen Sprache.* Berlin: Hertz, 1881.

Burn, A. R. *The Romans in Britain: An Anthology of Inscriptions.* 2nd ed. Columbia, S. C.: University of South Carolina Press, 1969.

Carnoy, Albert J. *Le Latin d'Espagne d'après les inscriptions.* 2nd ed. Louvain: J. B. Istas, 1906.

Collart, Jean. *Histoire de la langue latine.* Paris: Presses Universitaires, 1967.

Collingwood, R. G., and Myres, J.N.L. *Roman Britain and the English Settlements.* 2nd ed. The Oxford History of England. Oxford: Clarendon Press, 1963.

Colombis, Antonio. "Elementi veglioti nell'isola di Cherso-Ossero." *Archivum Romanicum,* XXI (1911), 75-116.

Densusianu, Ovide. *Histoire de la langue roumaine.* Vol. I. Paris: Ernest Leroux, 1901.

Devoto, Giacomo. *Storia della lingua di Roma.* Istituto di studi romani, Vol. XXIII. Bologna: Licinio Cappelli, 1940.

Díaz y Díaz, Manuel C. *Antología del latin vulgar.* 2nd ed. Biblioteca Románica Hispánica. Madrid: Editorial Gredos, 1962.

Elcock, W. D. *The Romance Languages.* London: Faber and Faber, 1960.

Fergusson, T. "A History of the Romance Vowel Systems Through Paradigmatic Reconstruction." Unpublished Ph. D. Dissertation, Department of French and Romance Philology, Columbia University, 1970.

Friedwanger, Matthias. "Über die Sprache and Heimat der Rumänen." *Zeitschrift fur romanische Philologie,* 54 (1934), 641-715.

Gaeng, Paul A. *An Inquiry into Local Variations in Vulgar Latin as Reflected in the Vocalism of Christian Inscriptions.* University of North Carolina Studies in the Romance Languages and Literatures, No. 77. Chapel Hill: University of North Carolina Press, 1968.

Goff, E. M. "The Language of the Eighth-Century Documents in Central Italy." Unpublished Ph.D. Dissertation, Department of French and Romance Philology, Columbia University, 1958.

Grandgent, C. H. *An Introduction to Vulgar Latin.* 1907; rpt. New York: Hafner, 1962.

———. *From Latin to Italian.* Cambridge, 1940.

Guiraud, Pierre. *Problèmes et méthodes de la statistique linguistique.* Paris: Presses Universitaires de France, 1960.

Hadlich, Roger L. "The Phonological History of Vegliote." University of North Carolina Studies in the Romance Languages and Literatures, No. 52. Chapel Hill: University of North Carolina Press, 1965.

Hall, Robert A., Jr. "The Reconstruction of Proto-Romance." *Language,* 26 (1950), 6-27.

Hanslik, Rudolf. Review of *Limba latină in provinciile dunărene ale imperiului român,* by H. Mihăescu. *Kratylos,* 10 (1965), 211-13.

Haudricourt, A. G., and Juilland, A. G. *Essai pour une histoire structurale du phonétisme français.* Paris: Klincksieck, 1949.

Herman, J. "Aspects de la différenciation territoriale du latin sous l'Empire." *Bulletin de la Société de Linguistique de Paris*, 60 (1965), 53-70.
Hoffmann, Ernst. *De Titulis Africae Latinis Quaestiones Phoneticae*. Diss. Breslau, 1907. Breslau: Robert Noske, 1907.
Hofman, J. B. *Lateinische Umgangssprache*. 3rd ed. Indogermanische Bibliothek. Heidelberg: Carl Winter, 1951.
Iordan, Iorgu. *Lingüistica románica*. Trans. Manuel Alvar. Madrid: Ediciones Alcalá, 1967.
Jackson, Kenneth. *Language and History in Early Britain*. Edinburgh: Edinburgh University Press, 1953.
──────. "On the Vulgar Latin of Roman Britain," in *Medieval Studies in honor of Jeremiah Denis Matthias Ford*, ed. Urban T. Holmes, Jr., and Alex J. Denomy, C.S.B. Cambridge, Mass.: Harvard University Press, 1948, pp. 83-103.
Jeanneret, Maurice. *La Langue des tablettes d'exécration latines*. Diss. Neuchatel, 1916. Paris: Attinger Frères, 1918.
Jochnowitz, George. *Dialect Boundries and the Question of Franco-Provençal*. The Hague: Mouton, 1973.
Jungemann, Fredrick H. *La teoría del sustrato y los dialectos hispano-romances y gascones*. Trans. D. Emilio Alarcos Llorach. Madrid: Editorial Gredos, 1955.
Knott, Betty. "The Christian 'Special Language' in the Inscriptions." *Vigilae Christianae*, X (1956), 65-79.
Kroll, W. "Das afrikanische Latein." *Rheinisches Museum für Philologie*, 52 (1897), 569-90.
Kübler, Bernhard. "Die lateinische Sprache auf afrikanischen Inschriften." *Archiv für lateinische Lexikographie und Grammatik*, 8 (1893), 161-202.
Kuhn, Alwin. *Die romanischen Sprachen*. Vol. I. Bern: A. Francke, 1951.
Lausberg, Heinrich. *Lingüistica románica*. 2 vols. Trans. J. Pérez Riesco and E. Pascual Rodríguez. Biblioteca Románica Hispánica. Madrid: Editorial Gredos, 1966.
LeBlant Edmond. *L'Épigraphie chrétienne en Gaule et dans l'Afrique romane*. Paris: Ernest Leroux, 1890.
Lindsay, W. M. *The Latin Language*. Oxford: Clarendon Press, 1894.
Löfstedt, Bengt. *Studien über die Sprache der langobardischen Gesetze*. Uppsala: Almquist and Wilksells, 1961.
Löfstedt, Einar. *Late Latin*. Oslo: Aschehoug, 1959.
Lot, F. "A quelle époque a-t-on cessé de parler latin?" *Archivum Latinitatis Medii Aevi*, VI (1931), 97-159.
Loth, J. *Les Mots latins dans les langues brittaniques*. Paris: Émile Bouillon, 1892.
Maccarrone, Nunzio. "Il latino delle iscrizioni di Sicilia." *Studi romanzi*, 7 (1911), 75-116.
Martinet, André. *Économie des changements phonétiques*. Berne: A. Francke, 1955.
──────. "Some Problems of Italic Consonantism." *Word*, 6 (1953), 26-35.
Maurer, Theodoro Henrique, Jr. *Gramática do Latim Vulgar*. Rio de Janeiro: Livraria Academica, 1959.
──────. *O Problema do Latim Vulgar*. Rio de Janeiro: Livraria Academica, 1962.
Menéndez-Pidal, Ramón. *Manual de gramática histórica española*. 10th ed. Madrid: Espasa-Calpe, 1958.

Menéndez-Pidal, Ramón. *Orígenes del español.* 4th ed. Madrid: Espasa-Calpe, 1956.

Meyer-Lübke, W. *Grammatica Storica della lingua italiana e dei dialetti toscani.* Trans. Matteo Bartoli e Giacomo Braun. Torino: Loescher Editore, 1964.

Mihăescu, H. *Limba latină în provinciile dunărene ale imperiului român.* Comisia pentru studiul formării limbii și poporului romîn, Vol. III. Bucharest: Editura Academiei Republicii Populare Romîne, 1960.

Miles, George C. *The Coinage of the Visigoths in Spain from Leovigild to Achila II.* New York: American Numismatic Society, 1952.

Mohl, Friedrich G. *Introduction à la chronologie du latin vulgaire.* Bibliothèque de l'École des Hautes Études Sciences philologiques et historiques, Fasc. 122. Paris: E. Bouillon, 1899.

Mohrmann, Christine. *Études sur le latin des chrétiens.* 3 vols. Rome: Edizioni di Storia e Letteratura, 1961-65.

―――. *Latin vulgaire, latin des chrétiens, latin médiéval.* Paris: Klincksieck, 1955.

Muller, Henri F. "A Chronology of Vulgar Latin." *Zeitschrift für romanische Philologie,* Beihaft 78. Halle: Max Niemeyer, 1929.

Navarro Tomás, T. *Manual de pronunciación española* (Publicaciones de la Revista de Filología Española, No. 3). 9th ed. Madrid: 1959.

Niedermann, Max. *Précis de phonétique historique du latin.* 4th ed. Paris: Klincksieck, 1953.

Odenkirchen, Carl J. "The Consonantism of Later Latin Inscriptions: A Contribution to the 'Vulgar Latin' Question." Unpublished Ph.D. Dissertation, Department of Romance Languages and Literatures, University of North Carolina, 1952.

Omeltchenko, S. W. "A Quantitative-Comparative Study of the Vocalism of the Latin Inscriptions from North Africa, Britain, Dalmatia and the Balkans." Unpublished Ph.D. Dissertation, Department of French and Romance Philology, Columbia University, 1971.

Palmer, Leonard R. *The Latin Language.* London: Faber and Faber, 1954.

Parodi, E. "Del Passagio di *v-* in *b-* e di certe perturbazioni delle leggi fonetiche nel latino vulgare." *Romania,* XXVII (1898), 177-240.

Pauly, August Friedrich von. *Paulys Real-Encyclopädie der Altertumswissenschaft. Neue Bearbeitung.* Herausgegeben von Georg Wissowa. Band IV. Stuttgart: J. B. Metzier, 1901.

Pei, Mario A. "Intervocalic Occlusives in 'East' and 'West' Romance." *The Romanic Review,* XXXIV (1943), 235-47.

―――. *The Italian Language.* 2nd ed. New York: S. F. Vanni, 1954.

―――. *The Language of the Eighth-Century Texts in Northern France.* New York: Carranza and Co., Inc., 1932.

Pirson, Jules, *La Langue des inscriptions latines de la Gaule,* Bibliothèque de la Faculté de Philosophie & Lettres de l'Université de Liège, Fascicule XI. Bruxelles, 1901.

Pisani, Vittore. *Testi latini arcaici e volgari con commento glottologico.* 2nd ed. revised Torino: Rosenberg and Sellfer, 1950.

Pogatscher, Alois. *Zur Lautlehre der griechischen, lateinischen, romanischen Lehnworte im Altenglischen.* Quellen und Forshungen zur Sprach- und Culturgeschichte der germanischen Völker, Vol. LXIV. Strassburg: Karl J. Trübner, 1888.

Politzer, Robert. "A Note on the North Italian Voicing of Intervocalic Stops." *Word*, 8 (1952), 211-214.

―――. "On the Chronology of the Simplification of Geminates in Northern France." *Modern Language Notes*, LXVI (1951), 527-531.

―――. "On *b* and *v* in Latin and Romance," *Word*, 8 (1952) 211-215.

―――. "On the Development of Latin Stops in Aragonese." *Word*, 10 (1954), 60-65.

―――. "On the Fall of Latin *-b-* in Rumanian and Related Phenomena." *Acta Lingüística*, 7 (1952), 32-39.

―――. *A Study of the Language of the Eighth Century Lombardic Documents*. New York: 1949.

Pope, M. K. *From Latin to Modern French with Especial Consideration of Anglo-Norman*. Manchester University Press, 1934.

Posner, Rebecca. *The Romance Languages: A Linguistic Introduction*. Anchor Books. New York: Doubleday, 1966.

Pulgram, Ernst. "Spoken and Written Latin." *Language*, 26 (1950), 458-66.

―――. *The Tongues of Italy*. Cambridge, Mass.: Harvard University Press, 1958.

Pușcariu, Sextil. *Études de linguistique roumaine*. Cluj-Bucharest: Imprimeria Națională, 1937.

Richter, Elise. "Beiträge zur Geschichte der Romanismen: Chronologische Phonetik des Französischen bis zum Ende des 8. Jahrhunderts." *Zeitschrift für romanische Philologie*, Beiheft 82. Halle: Max Niemeyer, 1934.

Rohlfs, Gerhard. *Historische Grammatik der italienischen Sprache und ihrer Mundarten*. 3 vols. Bibliotheca Románica, Series prima: Manualia et Commentationes, V-VII. Bern: A. Francke, 1949-54.

―――. *Romanische Philologie*. I. 2nd ed. Heidelberg: Carl Winter, 1966. II. Heidelberg: Carl Winter, 1952.

―――. *Vom Vulgärlatein zum Altfranzösischen*. Sammlung kurzer Lehrbucher der romanischen Sprachen und Literaturen, No. 15. Tübingen: Max Niemeyer, 1960.

Rosenkranz, Bernhard. "Die Gliederung des Dalmatischen." *Zeitschrift für romanische Philologie*, 71 (1955), 269-79.

Rosetti, Al. *Istoria limbii romine*. 3 vols. 4th ed. Bucharest: Editura Ştlințifica, 1964.

Russu, I. I. Review of *Limba latină in provinciile dunărene ale imperiului român*, by H. Mihăescu. *Cercetări de Lingvistică*. 6 (1961), 209-18.

Sandfeld, Kristian. *Linguistique balkanique*. La Société de Linguistique de Paris, XXXI. Paris. E. Champion, 1930.

Schiaffini Alfredo. "Problemi del passagio dal latino all'italiano (evoluzioni, disgregazioni, ricostruzioni)," *Studi in onore di Angelo Monteverdi*, Modena, Società tipografica editrice modenese, 1959, pp. 691-715.

Schmeck, Helmut. *Aufgaben und Methoden der modernen vulgärlateinischen Forschung*. Heidelberg: Carl Winter, 1955.

Schrijnen, Jos. *Charakteristik des altchristlichen Lateins*. Latinitas Christianorum Primaeva. Fasciculus Primus. Nijmegen: Dekker and van de Vegt, 1932.

Schuchardt, Hugo. *Der Vokalismus des Vulgärlateins*. 3 vols. Leipzig: B. G. Tuebner, 1866-68.

Silva Neto, Serafim da. *História do latim vulgar*. Biblioteca Brasileira de Filologia, No. 13. Rio de Janeiro: Livraria Academica, 1957.
Sittl, Karl. *Die lokalen Verschiedenheiten der lateinischen Sprache mit besonderer Berücksichtigung des afrikanischen Lateins*. Erlangen: Andreas Deichert, 1882.
Skok, Petar. *Pojave vulgarno-latinskoga jezika na natpisima rimske provincije Dalmacije*. Jugoslavenska Akademija Znanosti i Umjetnosti, Vol. XXV. Zagreb: Hartman, 1915.
———. "Zum Balkanlatein." *Zeitschrift für romanische Philologie*, 48 (1928), 398-403; 50 (1930), 484-532; 54 (1934), 175-215, 424-99.
Soderstrom Gunnar. *Epigraphica Latina Africana*. Diss. Uppsala, 1924. Uppsala: Appelbergs Boktryckeri, 1924.
Sofer, Johann. "Die Differenzierung der romanischen Sprachen." *Die Sprache*, II (1950-52), 23-28.
———. *Zur Problematik des Vulgärlateins: Ergebnisse und Anregungen*. Vienna: Gerold, 1963.
Sommer, Ferdinand. *Handbuch der lateinischen Laut- und Formenlehre*. 2nd and 3rd eds. Heidelberg: Carl Winter, 1948.
Stati, Sorin. Review of *Limba latină in provinciile dunărene ale imperiului român*, by H. Mihăescu. *Studii şi Cercetari Lingvistice*, 4 (1960), 957-63.
Stolz, Friedrich, and Debrunner, Albert. *Geschichte der lateinischen Sprache*. 4th ed. revised by Wolfgang P. Schmid. Sammlung Goschen, Band 492/492a. Berlin: Walter de Gruyter, 1966.
Straka, Georges. "La dislocation linguistique de la Romania et la formation des langues romanes à la lumière de la chronologie relative des changements phonétiques." *Revue de Linguistique Romane*, XX (1956), 249-57.
———. Review of *Limba latină in provinciile dunărene ale imperiului român*, by H. Mihăescu. *Revue de Linguistique Romane*, XXIV (1960), 403-06.
Strecker, Karl. *Introduction à l'étude du latin médiéval*. 3rd ed. Trans. Paul van de Woestijne. Société de Publications Romanes et Françaises, XXVI. Geneva: Librairie Droz, 1939.
Sturtevant, Edgar H. *The Pronunciation of Greek and Latin*. 2nd ed. Philadelphia: Linguistic Society of America, 1940.
Sylloga Inscriptionum Christianarum Veterum Musei Vaţicani, edited by Henrico Zilliacus. 2 vols. Acta Instituti Romani Finlandiae. Helsinki: Tilgmann, 1963.
Tagliavini, Carlo. "Dalmatica, Lingua." *Enciclopedia Italiana*. Rome: Istituto Giovanni Treccani, 1931.
———. *Le origini delle lingue neolatine*. 3rd ed. Bologna: Patron, 1962.
Terracini, A. "Di che cosa fanno la storia gli storici del linguaggio? Storia dei tipi *Benio* e *Nerba* nel latino volgare." *Acta Glottalogico Italiano*, 27 (1935), 133-152; 28 (1936), 1-31, 134-50.
Tiktin, Hariton. *Rumänisches Elementarbuch*. Heidelberg: C. Winter, 1905.
———. "Die rumänische Sprache." *Grundriss der romanischen Philologie*. Ed. Gustav Gröber. Strassburg: Karl J. Trubner, 1904-06. I, 564-607.
Tovar, Antonio. "A Research Report on Vulgar Latin and Its Local Variations." *Kratylos*, 9 (1964), 113-34.
Väänänen, Veikko. *Le Latin vulgaire des inscriptions pompéiennes*. 2nd ed. Abhandlungen der deutschen Akademie der Wissenschaften zu Berlin, No. 3. Berlin: Akademie-Verlag, 1959.

Väänänen, Veikko. *Introduction au latin vulgaire*. Bibliothèque Française et Romane, Série A: Manuels et Études Linguistiques, 6. Paris: Klincksieck, 1967.

―――. Review of *Die Sprache der longobardischen Gesetze*, by B. Lofstedt *Neuphilologische Mitteilungen*, LXII (1961), 221-26.

Vidos, B. E. *Manuale di linguistica romanza*. Trans. G. Francescato. Biblioteca dell' "Archivum Romanicum." Serie II. *Linguistica*, Vol. 28. Geneva: Olschki, 1959.

Vossler, Karl. *Einführung ins Vulgärlatein*. Herausgegeben und beabeitet von Helmut Schmeck. Munich: Max Hueber, 1953.

Wagner, Max Leopold. "Historische Lautlehre des Sardischen." *Zeitschrift für romanische Philologie*, Beiheft 90. Halle: Max Niemeyer, 1941.

―――. *La lingua sarda: storia, spirito e forma*. Bibliotheca Romanica, Series prima, Manualia et Commentationes, III. Bern: A. Francke, 1951.

―――. "Lautlehre der südsardischen Mundarten." *Zeitschrift für romanische Philologie*, Beiheft 12. Halle: Max Niemeyer, 1907.

Wartburg, Walther von. *Die Ausgliederung der romanischen Sprachräume*. Bibliotheca Romanica, Series prima, Manualia et Commentationes, VIII. Bern: A. Francke, 1950.

―――. *Les Origines des peuples romans*. Trans. Claude Cuenot de Maupassant. Paris: Presses Universitaires de France, 1941.

―――. *Problèmes et méthodes de la linguistique*. 2nd ed. Trans. Pierre Maillard. Paris: Presses Universitaires de France, 1963.

Weinrich, Harald. *Phonologische Studien zur romanischen Sprachgeschichte*. Forschungen zur romanischen Philologie, Heft 6. Münster, Westfalen: Aschendorffsche, 1958.

Zamora Vicente, Alonso. *Dialectología española*. Madrid: Editorial Gredos, 1960.

Reference Grammars and Dictionaries

Allen and Greenough's *New Latin Grammar*, ed. J. B. Greenough, G. L. Kettredge, A. A. Howard, and Benj. L. D'Ooge. Revised edition. Boston: Ginn and Company, 1916.

DuCange, D. D. *Glossarium Mediae et Infimae Latinitatis*. 8 vols. 1883-87; reprint. Graz: Akademische Druk- u. Verlagsanstalt, 1954.

Hale, William Gardner, and Buck, Carl Darling. *A Latin Grammar*. Alabama Linguistic and Philological Series, No. 8. 1903: reprint. Alabama: University of Alabama Press, 1966.

Harper's Latin Dictionary: A New Latin Dictionary Founded on The Translation of Freund's Latin-German Lexicon. Ed. E. A. Andres. Revised, enlarged, and in great part rewritten by Charles T. Lewis and Charles Short. New York: American Book Company, 1907.

Meyer-Lübke, W. *Romanisches etymologisches Wörterbuch*. 3rd ed. Heidelberg: Carl Winter, 1935.

Thesaurus Linguae Latinae. Leipzig: B. G. Teübner, since 1900.

NORTH CAROLINA STUDIES IN THE ROMANCE LANGUAGES AND LITERATURES

I.S.B.N. Prefix 0-8078-

Recent Titles

STUDIES IN HONOR OF ALFRED G. ENGSTROM, edited by Robert T. Cargo and Emmanuel J. Mickel, Jr. 1972. (No. 124). *-924-3.*

A CRITICAL EDITION WITH INTRODUCTION AND NOTES OF GIL VICENTE'S "FLORESTA DE ENGANOS," by Constantine Christopher Stathatos. 1972. (No. 125). *-925-1.*

LI ROMANS DE WITASSE LE MOINE. *Roman du treizième siècle.* Édité d'après le manuscrit, fonds français 1553, de la Bibliothèque Nationale, Paris, par Denis Joseph Conlon. 1972. (No. 126). *-926-X.*

EL CRONISTA PEDRO DE ESCAVIAS. *Una vida del Siglo XV,* por Juan Bautista Avalle-Arce. 1972. (No. 127). *-927-8.*

AN EDITION OF THE FIRST ITALIAN TRANSLATION OF THE "CELESTINA," by Kathleen V. Kish. 1973. (No. 128). *-928-6.*

MOLIÈRE MOCKED. THREE CONTEMPORARY HOSTILE COMEDIES: *Zélinde, Le portrait du peintre, Elomire Hypocondre,* by Frederick Wright Vogler. 1973. (No. 129). *-929-4.*

C.-A. SAINTE-BEUVE. *Chateaubriand et son groupe littéraire sous l'empire.* Index alphabétique et analytique établi par Lorin A. Uffenbeck. 1973. (No. 130). *-930-8.*

THE ORIGINS OF THE BAROQUE CONCEPT OF "PEREGRINATIO," by Juergen Hahn. 1973. (No. 131). *-931-6.*

THE "AUTO SACRAMENTAL" AND THE PARABLE IN SPANISH GOLDEN AGE LITERATURE, by Donald Thaddeus Dietz. 1973. (No. 132). *-932-4.*

FRANCISCO DE OSUNA AND THE SPIRIT OF THE LETTER, by Laura Calvert. 1973. (No. 133). *-933-2.*

ITINERARIO DI AMORE: DIALETTICA DI AMORE E MORTE NELLA VITA NUOVA, by Margherita de Bonfils Templer. 1973. (No. 134). *-934-0.*

L'IMAGINATION POÉTIQUE CHEZ DU BARTAS: ELEMENTS DE SENSIBILITE BAROQUE DANS LA "CREATION DU MONDE," by Bruno Braunrot. 1973. (No. 135). *-934-0.*

ARTUS DESIRE: PRIEST AND PAMPHLETEER OF THE SIXTEENTH CENTURY, by Frank S. Giese. 1973. (No. 136). *-936-7.*

JARDIN DE NOBLES DONZELLAS, FRAY MARTIN DE CORDOBA, by Harriet Goldberg. 1974. (No. 137). *-937-5.*

MYTHE ET PSYCHOLOGIE CHEZ MARIE DE FRANCE DANS "GUIGEMAR", par Antoinette Knapton. 1975. (No. 142). *-942-1.*

THE LYRIC POEMS OF JEHAN FROISSART: A CRITICAL EDITION, by Rob Roy McGregor, Jr. 1975. (No. 143). *-943-X.*

THE HISPANO-PORTUGUESE CANCIONERO OF THE HISPANIC SOCIETY OF AMERICA, by Arthur Askins. 1974. (No. 144). *-944-8.*

HISTORIA Y BIBLIOGRAFÍA DE LA CRÍTICA SOBRE EL "POEMA DE MÍO CID" (1750-1971), por Miguel Magnotta. 1976. (No. 145). *-945-6.*

LES ENCHANTEMENZ DE BRETAIGNE. AN EXTRACT FROM A THIRTEENTH CENTURY PROSE ROMANCE "LA SUITE DU MERLIN", edited by Patrick C. Smith. 1977. (No. 146). *-9146-0.*

THE DRAMATIC WORKS OF ÁLVARO CUBILLO DE ARAGÓN, by Shirley B. Whitaker. 1975. (No. 149). *-949-9.*

A CONCORDANCE TO THE "ROMAN DE LA ROSE" OF GUILLAUME DE LORRIS, by Joseph R. Danos. 1976. (No. 156). *0-88438-403-9.*

When ordering please cite the *ISBN Prefix* plus the last four digits for each title.

NORTH CAROLINA STUDIES IN THE ROMANCE LANGUAGES AND LITERATURES

I.S.B.N. Prefix 0-8078-

Recent Titles

POETRY AND ANTIPOETRY: A STUDY OF SELECTED ASPECTS OF MAX JACOB'S POETIC STYLE, by Annette Thau. 1976. (No. 158). *-005-X.*

FRANCIS PETRARCH, SIX CENTURIES LATER, by Aldo Scaglione. 1975. (No. 159).

STYLE AND STRUCTURE IN GRACIÁN'S "EL CRITICÓN", by Marcia L. Welles, 1976. (No. 160). *-007-6.*

MOLIERE: TRADITIONS IN CRITICISM, by Laurence Romero. 1974 (Essays, No. 1). *-001-7.*

CHRÉTIEN'S JEWISH GRAIL. A NEW INVESTIGATION OF THE IMAGERY AND SIGNIFICANCE OF CHRÉTIEN DE TROYES'S GRAIL EPISODE BASED UPON MEDIEVAL HEBRAIC SOURCES, by Eugene J. Weinraub. 1976. (Essays, No. 2). *-002-5.*

STUDIES IN TIRSO, I, by Ruth Lee Kennedy. 1974. (Essays, No. 3). *-003-3.*

VOLTAIRE AND THE FRENCH ACADEMY, by Karlis Racevskis. 1975. (Essays, No. 4). *-004-1.*

THE NOVELS OF MME RICCOBONI, by Joan Hinde Stewart. 1976. (Essays, No. 8). *-008-4.*

FIRE AND ICE: THE POETRY OF XAVIER VILLAURRUTIA, by Merlin H. Forster. 1976. (Essays, No. 11). *-011-4.*

THE THEATER OF ARTHUR ADAMOV, by John J. McCann. 1975. (Essays, No. 13). *-013-0.*

AN ANATOMY OF POESIS: THE PROSE POEMS OF STÉPHANE MALLARMÉ, by Ursula Franklin. 1976. (Essays, No. 16). *-016-5.*

LAS MEMORIAS DE GONZALO FERNÁNDEZ DE OVIEDO, Vols. I and II, by Juan Bautista Avalle-Arce. 1974. (Texts, Textual Studies, and Translations, Nos. 1 and 2). *-401-2; 402-0.*

GIACOMO LEOPARDI: THE WAR OF THE MICE AND THE CRABS, translated, introduced and annotated by Ernesto G. Caserta. 1976. (Texts, Textual Studies, and Translations, No. 4). *-404-7.*

LUIS VÉLEZ DE GUEVARA: A CRITICAL BIBLIOGRAPHY, by Mary G. Hauer. 1975. (Texts, Textual Studies, and Translations, No. 5). *-405-5.*

UN TRÍPTICO DEL PERÚ VIRREINAL: "EL VIRREY AMAT, EL MARQUÉS DE SOTO FLORIDO Y LA PERRICHOLI". EL "DRAMA DE DOS PALANGANAS" Y SU CIRCUNSTANCIA. estudio preliminar, reedición y notas por Guillermo Lohmann Villena. 1976. (Texts, Textual Studies, and Translation, No. 15). *-415-2.*

LOS NARRADORES HISPANOAMERICANOS DE HOY, edited by Juan Bautista Avalle-Arce. 1973. (Symposia, No. 1). *-951-0.*

ESTUDIOS DE LITERATURA HISPANOAMERICANA EN HONOR A JOSÉ J. ARROM, edited by Andrew P. Debicki and Enrique Pupo-Walker. 1975. (Symposia, No. 2). *-952-9.*

MEDIEVAL MANUSCRIPTS AND TEXTUAL CRITICISM, edited by Christopher Kleinhenz. 1976. (Symposia, No. 4). *-954-5.*

SAMUEL BECKETT. THE ART OF RHETORIC, edited by Edouard Morot-Sir, Howard Harper, and Dougald McMillan III. 1976. (Symposia, No. 5). *-955-3.*

DELIE. CONCORDANCE, by Jerry Nash. 1976. 2 Volumes. (No. 174).

FIGURES OF REPETITION IN THE OLD PROVENÇAL LYRIC: A STUDY IN THE STYLE OF THE TROUBADOURS, by Nathaniel B. Smith. 1976. (No. 176). *-9176-2.*

A CRITICAL EDITION OF LE REGIME TRESUTILE ET TRESPROUFITABLE POUR CONSERVER ET GARDER LA SANTE DU CORPS HUMAIN, by Patricia Willett Cummins. 1977. (No. 177).

THE DRAMA OF SELF IN GUILLAUME APOLLINAIRE'S "ALCOOLS", by Richard Howard Stamelman. 1976. (No. 178). *-9178-9.*

When ordering please cite the *ISBN Prefix* plus the last four digits for each title.

NORTH CAROLINA STUDIES IN THE ROMANCE LANGUAGES AND LITERATURES.

I.S.B.N. Prefix 0-8078-

Recent Titles

A CRITICAL EDITION OF "LA PASSION NOSTRE SEIGNEUR" FROM MANUSCRIPT 1131 FROM THE BIBLIOTHEQUE SAINTE-GENEVIEVE, PARIS, by Edward J. Gallagher. 1976. (No. 179). *-9179-7.*
A QUANTITATIVE AND COMPARATIVE STUDY OF THE VOCALISM OF THE LATIN INSCRIPTIONS OF NORTH AFRICA, BRITAIN, DALMATIA, AND THE BALKANS, by Stephen William Omeltchenko. 1977. (No. 180). *-9180-0.*
OCTAVIEN DE SAINT-GELAIS "LE SEJOUR D'HONNEUR", edited by Joseph A. James. 1977. (No. 181). *-9181-9.*
A STUDY OF NOMINAL INFLECTION IN LATIN INSCRIPTIONS, by Paul A. Gaeng. 1977. (No. 182). *-9182-7.*
THE LIFE AND WORKS OF LUIS CARLOS LÓPEZ, by Martha S. Bazik. 1977. (No. 183). *-9183-5.*
"THE CORT D'AMOR". A THIRTEENTH-CENTURY ALLEGORICAL ART OF LOVE, by Lowanne E. Jones. 1977. (No. 185). *-9185-1.*
PHYTONYMIC DERIVATIONAL SYSTEMS IN THE ROMANCE LANGUAGES: STUDIES IN THEIR ORIGIN AND DEVELOPMENT, by Walter E. Geiger. 1978. (No. 187). *-9187-8.*
LANGUAGE IN GIOVANNI VERGA'S EARLY NOVELS, by Nicholas Patruno. 1977. (No. 188). *-9188-6.*
BLAS DE OTERO EN SU POESÍA, by Moraima de Semprún Donahue. 1977. (No. 189). *-9189-4.*
LA ANATOMÍA DE "EL DIABLO COJUELO": DESLINDES DEL GÉNERO ANATOMÍSTICO, por C. George Peale. 1977. (No. 191). *-9191-6.*
RICHARD SANS PEUR, EDITED FROM "LE ROMANT DE RICHART" AND FROM GILLES CORROZET'S "RICHART SANS PAOUR", by Denis Joseph Conlon. 1977. (No. 192). *-9192-4.*
MARCEL PROUST'S GRASSET PROOFS. *Commentary and Variants,* by Douglas Alden. 1978. (No. 193). *-9193-2.*
MONTAIGNE AND FEMINISM, by Cecile Insdorf. 1977. (No. 194). *-9194-0.*
SANTIAGO F. PUGLIA, AN EARLY PHILADELPHIA PROPAGANDIST FOR SPANISH AMERICAN INDEPENDENCE, by Merle S. Simmons. 1977. (No. 195). *-9195-9.*
BAROQUE FICTION-MAKING. A STUDY OF GOMBERVILLE'S "POLEXANDRE", by Edward Baron Turk. 1978. (No. 196). *-9196-7.*
THE TRAGIC FALL: DON ÁLVARO DE LUNA AND OTHER FAVORITES IN SPANISH GOLDEN AGE DRAMA, by Raymond R. MacCurdy. 1978. (No. 197). *-9197-5.*
A BAHIAN HERITAGE. An Ethnolinguistic Study of African Influences on Bahian Portuguese, by William W. Megenney. 1978. (No. 198). *-9198-3.*
"LA QUERELLE DE LA ROSE: Letters and Documents", by Joseph L. Baird and John R. Kane. 1978. (No. 199). *-9199-1.*
TWO AGAINST TIME. *A Study of the very present worlds of Paul Claudel and Charles Péguy,* by Joy Nachod Humes. 1978. (No. 200). *-9200-9.*
TECHNIQUES OF IRONY IN ANATOLE FRANCE. Essay on *Les sept femmes de la Barbe-Bleue,* by Diane Wolfe Levy. 1978. (No. 201). *-9201-7.*
THE PERIPHRASTIC FUTURES FORMED BY THE ROMANCE REFLEXES OF "VADO (AD)" "PLUS INFINITIVE, by James Joseph Champion. 1978 (No. 202). *-9202-5.*
THE EVOLUTION OF THE LATIN /b/-/ʮ/ MERGER: A Quantitative and Comparative Analysis of the *B-V* Alternation in Latin Inscriptions, by Joseph Louis Barbarino. 1978 (No. 203). *-9203-3.*
METAPHORIC NARRATION: THE STRUCTURE AND FUNCTION OF METAPHORS IN "A LA RECHERCHE DU TEMPS PERDU", by Inge Karalus Crosman. 1978 (No. 204). *-9204-1.*

When ordering please cite the *ISBN Prefix* plus the last four digits for

The Department of Romance Studies Digital Arts and Collaboration Lab at the University of North Carolina at Chapel Hill is proud to support the digitization of the North Carolina Studies in the Romance Languages and Literatures series.